BULLY BLOCKING AT WORK

A Self-Help Guide for Employees and Managers

Evelyn M. Field

www.
AUSTRALIANACADEMICPRESS
.com.au

First published in 2010
Australian Academic Press
32 Jeays Street
Bowen Hills Qld 4006
Australia
www.australianacademicpress.com.au

National Library of Australia Cataloguing-in-Publication entry:

Author:	Field, Evelyn.
Title:	Bully blocking at work : a self-help guide for employees and managers / Evelyn M. Field.
ISBN:	9781921513442 (pbk.)
Subjects:	Bullying in the workplace.
	Bullying in the workplace--Prevention.
	Harassment.
	Discrimination in employment.
	Discrimination in employment--Prevention.
	Conflict management.
Dewey Number:	331.133

Cartoons by Matt Mawson. Cover designed by Andrea Rinarelli.
Back cover photograph by Timna Fried.
Typeset in Adobe Garamond 11.5pt by Australian Academic Press.

PEFC

PEFC/21-31-50
Promoting sustainable
forest management

Bullying is an evil of global proportions; pervasive in our schools, workplaces, and now in cyberspace, where anonymous bullies spread their venom undetected on innocent victims. Evelyn M. Field's masterful analysis of the ways we can help employees cope with and overcome workplace bullying and harassment is a welcome addition to our understanding of this injustice and wise ways to deal with it. *Bully Blocking at Work* is a must-read for employees and managers concerned about how to right this wrong.

Philip Zimbardo, PhD
Stanford University
Author of *The Lucifer Effect, Understanding How Good People Turn Evil*

Using a combination of plain talk, passion, real-life stories, humour, and practical advice, once again Australia's leading expert in bullying behaviour has combined years of clinical experience with meticulous research, to create an indispensable compendium on workplace bullying. Evelyn Field helps readers worldwide understand and confront bullying alone or within their workplace. Her book provides an objective, balanced and comprehensive approach which focuses upon respect and responsibility for everyone involved, from the manager, target, bully to the silent bystander. Essential reading!

Dr Michael Carr-Gregg, psychologist, Melbourne

Kudos to bully expert Evelyn Field for this helpful book that shows people how to confront abusive, unsafe, unproductive behaviour instead of retreating and withdrawing and allowing aggressive, manipulative individuals to make everyone around them miserable. This book features many 'I can use that today' techniques. Read it and reap!

Sam Horn, author of *Take the Bully by the Horns* and *Tongue Fu!*®, USA

Evelyn Field has captured the essence of a considerable body of scientific research about workplace bullying in her book. She presents the deeply harmful character of this workplace phenomenon without a doomsday outlook by providing sound advice to those most directly affected and those responsible for managing day-to-day workplace operations. A great book for people who believe they are being targeted, those struggling with how to manage bullying in their organisations, and those who want to be of help.

Pamela Lutgen-Sandvik, USA

Evelyn Field's *Bully Blocking at Work: A Self-Help Guide for Employees and Managers*, published by Australian Academic Press, is a must-read for targets of workplace bullying, human resources managers, employee wellness professionals and, in fact, every supervisor or manager of people. Field follows a refreshing collaborative approach and makes a case for early intervention in the case of workplace bullying. The book is an inspiring easy-read, and while supporting the target, it also advocates an understanding of the traumatic experience of workplace bullying. This book will definitely contribute to healing the workplace and offers hope for a healthy workplace to the target and the perpetrator.

Dr Susan Steinman, Workplace Dignity Institute, South Africa
www.worktrauma.org and correspondence: susan@worktrauma.org

Evelyn Field is a founding member of the National Centre Against Bullying. She has written extensively on the subject, both in relation to children and in the workplace. She has extensive clinical experience in dealing with problems arising from bullying and is a highly respected psychologist. In this book she concentrates upon workplace bullying, which is equally as insidious as the bullying of children. This book will provide an invaluable source for all who are affected by bullying and provides practical answers.

The Hon Alastair Nicholson, AO RFD QC

This book is a wonderful resource for anyone who is experiencing bullying or trying to manage a bully at work. As the years go by we are learning so much more about the nature and dynamics of bullying. Someone needed to write this book because practical solutions that shift the dynamics of power are hard to find. I would recommend this to anyone who has been bullied, knows a target, or is trying to manage a difficult workplace situation.

Hadyn Olsen, bullying consultant, www.wave.org.nz

Over the last 10 years, and increasingly so of the last 5 years, bullying has become a significant focus for employment and personal injury lawyers. People who have been subjected to bullying are increasingly turning to the law for remedies in respect of loss of employment, loss of promotional opportunities and loss of enjoyment of life as a result of psychological illness linked to bullying. Reading through Evelyn's book, I recognise many of the scenarios that are often described to me by my clients. I hope that this book will encourage people who experience bullying to adopt the many self-help strategies and support described and that they are able to overcome problems in their workplaces without ever experiencing the sort of trauma which I see when people, as a last resort, seek legal help. I also hope that by further identifying workplace bullying as a significant issue, we will encourage workplace cultures where bullying is not tolerated. While workplace laws dealing with bullying are probably in need of attention, prevention is a much more effective remedy.

David Shaw, Employment Law Partner, Holding Redlich, Melbourne

'Treat others as you would like them to treat you.'

To the Almighty,
Now I understand the path you made for me and thank you
for choosing me to undertake this journey.

To my mother Marianne Roth, my sister Vivienne Fried,
my special family and friends who are here with me now,
and to those who have moved on.

To Bufy and Harry, my pampered papillons,
who help me manage workplace bullying stories every day,
and exemplify nature's way of building resilience.

Special thanks to the experts — the clients whose experiences have provided
me with the insight to inspire me and continue writing this book so others
may benefit — as well as to all the ordinary, everyday heroes
who make this world a better place!

COMING SOON

STRATEGIES FOR
BULLY BLOCKING AT WORK
Evelyn M. Field

For further information go to
www.australianacademicpress.com.au

Contents

Preface

I have long been fascinated by how people socialise, relate and establish personal connections. This comes from my interest in shyness. I was a shy child myself, but as an adult I developed my social skills and learnt how to better deal with people both in my social and professional life. Unfortunately some of this learning was through tragedy. Following the traumatic loss of my daughter Miriam, I began mulling over how people relate and connect. This led me to developing a simple social skills model. As I had been working as a school counsellor for many years prior, I began incorporating the model into my work on shyness and school bullying. The model not only provided a structure, it also supported my commitment to enabling parents and schools to teach students survival and resilience in dealing with difficult, mean or cruel people. That conviction was also influenced by my family history. My grandfather was a professor in Germany in the 1930s when Hitler's anti-Semitic policies began to escalate. His cousins soon left Germany, and my grandmother Margaret also wanted to leave, but her husband felt safe; he trusted the German government and couldn't visualise that the life he had always known was now threatened by monumental change. After the infamous anti-Jewish Kristallnacht pogrom of 1938, the Gestapo hunted down my grandfather and imprisoned him for a week. He died soon afterwards from a burst ulcer. Marianne, my mother, then 17 years old, was aware of their imminent danger and sought a sponsor. She sailed to Australia a month before World War II began. Hans, her 16-year-old brother, sailed to England. My grandmother remained alone in Germany, was taken to the Warsaw ghetto, and died in a concentration camp. If my grandfather had listened to his family, he could have left Germany and survived. His wife, my grandmother, paid the ultimate price as a consequence of his inability to adapt to the changes around him before it was too late.

My first book, *Bully Busting,* was published in 1999 with fantastic media and public interest. Within a week though, I was hit with a solicitor's letter demanding I pulp the book! I had unknowingly used a similar title for my book as a trademark held by two teachers. I was dumbfounded and angry. The irony of feeling bullied by adults via legal demands at the very time we were helping bullied children was not lost on me. Eventually and without lawyers, an agreement was reached and *Bully Busting* sold over 23,000 copies. A revised edition, *Bully Blocking,* also a bestseller, was released in 2007.

The whole experience was an eye-opener. I felt devastated by its effects for several years but I was now aware of something far worse than school bullying — bullying by adults, co-workers, colleagues, or bosses — workplace bullying. Everywhere I went from then on I became aware of bullying stories, from casual encounters and overheard conversations, to clients, conferences and courtroom battles. It was a clear personal message — the universe was telling me to take on workplace bullying and learn how to empower employees. This was reinforced by a chance meeting at a conference on bullying in Queensland with Paul McCarthy, then a lecturer in management at Griffith University. Paul suggested I write another self-help book on bullying, but for the workplace instead of the schoolyard.

I began writing in 1999, sent off the first manuscript in 2001, and entered hospital the same day. Evidently, my red blood cells were trying to destroy each other and I was suffering multiple ailments, including spleenal lymphoma, autoimmune disorder and haemolytic anaemia. I realised then that it was unconsciously linked to all the negative emotions I was dredging up through my workplace bullying research. In any case, the sickness and medication didn't help my concentration, and when my publisher rejected the manuscript my writing career went on hold. A few years later, I tried again, but I still couldn't think clearly, let alone write. Eventually I enlisted the aid of a young writer, Fabiola, and began reworking some pages. A writing weekend in a grand old hotel in Queenscliff pushed the manuscript a little further along. In 2004 I attended a Maui Writers Retreat and Conference in Hawaii and was fortunate enough to be mentored by Sam Horn, the American author and speaker, who understood bullying and helped me discover my writing voice.

Upon my return home, I at first concentrated on revising my first book, *Bully Busting*, and then turned again to my manuscript on workplace bullying, sending out a reworked manuscript to a list of publishers. The inevitable publisher rejection slips began to mount up as the book's potential was repeatedly evaluated as too low. Fortunately, one publisher was different. Stephen May from Australian Academic Press recognised the manuscript's value immediately. Stephen was a psychologist himself before becoming a publisher and well understands the importance of workplace stress and the need to educate and assist ordinary workers to deal with psychological pressure. Working with Stephen has not only been a pleasure from a professional and personal perspective, but a major boost to the book's integrity.

Thus, like a good wine, this book has taken over ten years to develop. But its core message has always remained clear. While it is up to employers to provide a safe workplace, that responsibility can only go so far in reducing workplace stress. Many years of research, restructuring, education and intervention into schoolyard bullying have yet to significantly reduce such behaviour. We risk being as ineffective in reducing workplace bullying if we rely solely on others to do what we must do ourselves. It is very simple to teach a student how to block a bully, I do it all the time in my office. We need to focus on teaching social and emotional resilience to empower adults and children — helping them develop their own social survival skills to deal with the ups and downs of life.

Evelyn Margaret Field
2010

CHAPTER ONE

Introduction

"*I can't believe this is happening to me.***"**

"*Am I being bullied at work?***"**

Most people find it difficult to acknowledge when they are being bullied, when they witness someone else being bullied, or when they are doing the bullying themselves. Few understand that bullying is not tough management or an aggressive personality trait to be suffered. Workplace bullying is toxic. It is a unique, unbelievably soul-destroying abuse of power. It threatens an employee's health and wellbeing, and any workplace that condones or fosters bullying is dysfunctional and dangerous.

Everyone dreads being humiliated, rejected, vulnerable, and without social support yet these are the results of workplace bullying. It strikes at the heart of who we are; activating a primitive fear of exclusion by the tribe — of being abandoned — creating feelings of anger, shame and denial. Severe and unremitting bullying catapults the victim into such a damaging emotional state that it can lead to the breakdown of their very survival mechanisms.

I have worked as a psychologist for over 30 years and helped many different types of clients, including targets of schoolyard bullying and victims of criminal trauma. I have spent many hours listening to clients, conducting interviews, reading, speaking and writing about workplace bullying. Still, to this day every time I hear a workplace bullying story in my practice I am hit with a horrible feeling in the pit of my stomach. It's so awful I sometimes want to expel the story from my mind, and feel like running away.

Most people accept that children can be bullied at school, yet cannot comprehend that workplace bullying is far worse than school bullying, far more extensive, and a massive health and productivity burden for the workplace, employers and their employees. Tragically, we now see bullies abusing and intimidating their staff and underlings under the guise of management billed as entertainment. Endless 'reality' television programs parade before us a staggering range of people of all backgrounds with a unifying trait of throwing tantrums in public, verbal abuse, and the single-minded pursuit of their own goals, no matter what the cost to others.

No wonder then that four men were found culpable in 2010 in the suicide of a young waitress at a trendy café in central Melbourne, Australia, from constant bullying, and sentenced to hefty fines under that state's occupational health and safety laws.

Workplace bullying is a serious psychological issue that deserves the utmost attention by the health, management, and human resources sectors. Today, many mental health professionals fail to assess symptoms accurately; some diagnose and treat victims inappropriately and relate to them without empathy or professional respect. It is no wonder. There is little education for either those treating the problem, or those who can prevent it. Psychiatrists and psychologists have yet to develop accurate diagnoses and evidence-based treatments for targets of workplace bullying. Unfortunately, many cases of workplace bullying that are ignored or dealt with in ignorance spiral out of control into destructive conflicts, harming both the bully and the victim, as well as severely damaging the productivity and reputation of the organisation in which it occurred.

This book therefore aims to educate readers about the evil nature of workplace bullying; to help you understand its toxic, destructive impact on all employees — whether they are targets, bullies or onlookers — and provide advice for coping and confronting bullying, from both a personal and organisational perspective. I hope that its impact can create a new movement to help employees and employers reduce the hazards of workplace bullying and align modern work and behaviour practices with reconciliation, social inclusion and improving performance. The goal is to acknowledge, validate and create safe workplaces. This involves empowering everyone, including employers, managers, targets, bullies, bystanders and the public to use collaborative processes so that everyone benefits.

Sprinkled liberally throughout the pages to come are quotes from many people I have worked with over the years. These are the genuine voices of victims and bullies; managers, relatives, bystanders and friends. Their words help to emphasise the concepts discussed in the text as well as providing a source of commonality with the reader who has suffered a similar fate.

Sometimes it is the simple act of hearing another's pain and struggle that helps us take those important steps forward for our own survival. Remember though, if as you read the information and examples provided you feel too many traumatic memories or emotional stress is surfacing, that you can always return to it later. This book is designed to provide you with long-term support, so read some bits that seem relevant now and refer to it later as required.

I have intentionally refrained from overusing the term 'victim' in this book, preferring instead to use the descriptors 'target' to indicate someone who is the intended receiver of a campaign of bullying behaviour, and 'recipient' to indicate someone who has experienced bullying behaviour by virtue of being present at the time of a bully's outburst. Likewise, although men are more likely to be found bullying than women due to their greater representation in management and the workplace generally, throughout the book I refer to both genders to remind the reader that women bully too and that both men and women can be affected by bullying.

Finally, no matter what help you gain from reading this book, you must always use professional advice from legal, psychological or medical specialists where required. In those cases, remember to be as clear and objective as possible in communicating both your own needs and the circumstances and effects of the events you have been involved in and why you are seeking professional help.

CHAPTER TWO

What is workplace bullying?

❝I worked for over 15 years in a stimulating, inspiring arts complex. When I began, there was female bullying, which had been reported regularly to management. However, it escalated alarmingly when Nick, the new manager, arrived courtesy of company nepotism and began serial bullying myself and two others. He would scream, isolate us in his office, froth at the mouth and enjoy seeing us cry. 'How do I sack Alice?' he emailed me by mistake.

We followed the designated policy. The union was supportive, but to my horror, our co-workers did nothing, while human resources and senior management supported him and said, 'We have faith in him'. They labelled the bullying as 'personality differences' and exacerbated the situation by informing him of our continuing complaints. They called us 'troublemakers' but did nothing else. Clearly they were oblivious to his ongoing psychiatric condition which was later revealed in court.

Maybe I should have left this job, but as a single, older female, I'd lost the confidence to apply elsewhere. Besides, I was unaware of the insidious, toxic impact of his sociopathic behaviours on my health. I became depressed, overweight and my blood pressure increased. I began taking antidepressants. A month later I broke down, with an invisible, devastating, debilitating injury; one day my body wouldn't carry me to work.

After nine years of severe depression and trauma I'm just coping with the damage to my life by the bully, my employer and their insurance company. Though the bully eventually lost his job, I've not been vindicated, validated or received justice. When my case ends, I can't imagine how I will ever work again or trust an employer to provide a safe environment. **❞**

Throughout history people have been excluded, marginalised, abused or harassed at work. The Egyptian pharaohs attracted surrounding tribes and people to their building sites and slowly led them into slavery. Today, across the globe many employees are disempowered, their basic right to work and achieve is restricted, minimised and abused in the name of such labels as racism, apartheid, ethnicity, class, and political and religious beliefs.

For most of us however, the practice of bullying at work takes on a more insidious persona. We are often unaware of its presence until we feel its devastating toxic effects on our own emotions or witness the psychological carnage around us as a colleague suffers verbal abuse and mental torment. But surely this can't be something that serious? Shouldn't we all just expect some 'tough love' at work?

While playing pranks on young apprentices by sending them to the store for a left-handed screwdriver or striped paint is still regarded by many as fun, the hierarchical, autocratic structures of many of today's business, military, police, government, health, or education sectors make it easier to escalate teasing into bullying. Likewise, the financially lucrative hunting ground of modern litigation encourages bullying as part of an adversarial legal process, and bullying barristers are often selected for their skills of attack and ability to demolish their opponent and witnesses. Politics is also a haven for bullies. Politicians are attracted to the power it provides, like moths to a flame. There are many ritual games played inside Parliament, but the real, nasty bullying takes place in the back corridors of power, where people's reputations may be torn to shreds by rumour campaigns designed to eliminate opponents.

Across the world, in any industry, in small or large workplaces, bullying forms part of a pattern of workplace violence.[1] Every day, conscientious, skilled employees confront the 'churn and burn' culture. They are exposed, directly or indirectly, to abusive behaviours by incompetent bullies. Bullying is a silent, systemic dysfunction that is widespread in many workplaces and is becoming one of the fastest growing complaints of workplace stress and violence.

The term itself is still an ugly, unpopular word to be avoided, just as 'child sexual abuse' was a few decades ago. It's a feisty, gutsy, in-your-face type of expression. Most people hate using it at school or at work — although no-one has produced a better description. It includes many other

> # What is workplace bullying?
>
> - Workplace bullying involves the repetitive, prolonged abuse of power.
>
> - Unwelcome, unreasonable, escalating behaviours are aggressively directed at one or more workers and cause humiliation, offence, intimidation and distress.
>
> - It places your health, wellbeing, safety and career at risk, interferes with job performance, and creates a toxic working environment.
>
> - Workplace bullying can attack anyone, in any career, at any level, within any organisation, at any time.[2]

descriptors, such as harassment, workplace conflict, emotional abuse, incivility, aggression, social undermining, petty tyranny, mobbing,[3] social ostracism, intimidation, hazing,[4] offensive behaviours, occupational violence, and victimisation.

Subtle but dangerous — it's difficult to identify

A popular fable claims that if you put a frog in a pot of boiling water, it will jump out quickly, but if you place it in a pot of cold water and heat it slowly, the frog remains unaware and dies. Recently we have become more aware of bullied apprentices, unsafe initiation rites, sexual harassment and racial discrimination, but bullying covers many different behaviours; it ranges from the subtle to the overt, from the passive to aggressive. It can be extremely devious and manipulative, so that it is almost impossible to identify or estimate its true danger. It may be simple to identify one bully but not the others, such as the mob who join in, or management who remain passive.

Some workplace bullying behaviours appear innocuous and petty at first, making them difficult to explain to human resources staff and friends. As a target of bullying you might find it hard to believe what's happening to you. Confused and bewildered, you may question yourself. *Is it really bullying?* It's hard to label your manager as a bully, especially if *he's really nice* at other times, or behind her saccharine, sweet voice there's a *real bitch*. Perhaps you try to cope because you believe that it's not *that* bad, as others experience abuse that's far worse. Similar to domestic violence victims who remain loyal to their abusive partner, you may forgive the bully each time, or feel stuck because of a learned helplessness. You may think that by working harder you will negate the bullying or eventually make it stop. Beware though that regardless of why someone is bullying you, you can be seriously injured.

Surprisingly, the concept of people abusing one another at work is considered a new, confusing and threatening subject within the fields of psychology, management, and human resources. Most of us, however, are aware that work can be difficult, stressful, sometimes dangerous, temporary and competitive. We know the difference between a rough day, tough management, and abuse. However, physical threats, humiliating verbal abuse, criminal behaviours, sabotaging work performance or creating scapegoats to camouflage negligent and unethical behaviours isn't fair. You go to work to achieve a sense of satisfaction, work in a professional polite environment and get paid for a fair day's work. You don't go to your workplace to be abused, humiliated or injured. And yet for far too many of us that is a part of our working life in one job or another. Which is why most people don't understand exactly what workplace bullying involves, why it occurs or the extent of damage and injury it can inflict. Few can also identify that just like the canary down the coalmine, bullying is a warning sign of an incompetent, toxic workplace.[5]

The bullying behaviours continuum

There are many ways in which people abuse their power to bully others. They tend to begin with something seemingly harmless and unrestrained before moving towards more aggressive behaviours and outright verbal abuse, often following a rebuke or confrontation. The initial subtlety can mask the bullying behaviour and its impact. Sometimes there may be a few single but significant or serious incidents over an extended period of time, producing a cumulative impact. Some targets identify all the bullying behaviours towards them (see Bully behaviours continuum) while others are oblivious — for example, about toxic emails which spread malicious rumours — and others only notice when the behaviours escalate, become more vicious or affect their work. Some finally become fully conscious about what is happening to them when they can't cope or concentrate and can no longer pretend that it doesn't affect them.

Bullying behaviours continuum

Banter
Tease/taunt
Malicious gossip
Humiliation
Verbal attack
Nuisance behaviour
Sabotage work performance
Denial of professional opportunities
Isolation or exclusion
Set unreasonable goals
Discrimination/harassment
Perception distortions
Covert or overt threats
Cyber abuse
Micro-management
Mobbing
Retaliation
Damage to property
Physical violence
Murder

The key message is that bullying behaviours tend to increase over time, moving from subtle and ordinary to more overt, humiliating, aggressive behaviours. Bullies do this because they obtain satisfaction from the target's powerlessness, or can get away with their behaviours as no-one makes them accountable for them. Targets unwittingly may enable bullies by not implementing bully blocking strategies early.

Workplace bullying behaviours

According to research there are five main areas where bullying occurs. These can be used as a guideline for assessing bullying behaviours.[6]

1. Work-related

> For example: 'I was told to report to X and nobody else.'
> 'Nobody told me they'd changed the meeting.' 'They stopped all

my duties.' 'Each week she changes the goalposts.' 'He paid me as an executive but wouldn't let me do the work.' 'Women who do the dirty establishment work are bullied out while bully's mate gets the promotion and retires rich.' 'They misused the discipline process.'

2. Personal attacks

For example: 'My boss called me a "fucking nightmare, nobody likes you, you'll never get another job". He said things like, "You're working against our team. You can't handle criticism. You're oversensitive. You're a troublemaker. You're incompetent and overpaid. If this was up to me I wouldn't give you a dime".' 'My boss said, "Gee you'd be hot in the tub tonight". He said to me, "I wonder how low that necklace goes?" but his excuse was, "I'm just being friendly".' 'He stood over me pointing and shouting.' 'When I was an apprentice they hung me upside down, put my head in a noose and set fire to me.'

3. Social isolation

For example: 'I was sent to Coventry by workmates, they're too scared to be seen with me.' 'I'm excluded from work functions.' 'I'm not a union member, so I'm not allowed to sit with them at lunch.' 'No-one rang to see how I was.' 'The CEO is full of shit, they all cover their butts and excel in burying bullying.' 'They didn't believe me until others complained.' 'Everyone knows about you.'

4. Verbal threats

For example: 'I was told, "You support me on this and I'll protect you".' 'He complained about a mistake I made years ago.' 'The bully penalises you in performance reviews and warning letters.' 'Everyone who complained to Equal Opportunity about the university lost their job.' 'I was bullied out because I knew how they concocted the figures.' 'The threat was: "You'll be next".'

5. Spreading rumours

For example: 'Frank's not a team player.' 'Nina couldn't cope and left.' 'She couldn't balance the books.' 'Mary had a breakdown.' 'We don't need to include him, do we?' 'It's harder to disprove the half truths than their outright lies.' 'Bill is a troublemaker and runs to the union.' 'People have been complaining about you.'

Bullies abuse power

Bullying behaviours involve the regular abuse of power by a bully and an experienced loss of power by the target. Bullying cannot occur where both people feel equally powerful — that's called a conflict, which may be stressful but is not traumatic.

Bullies instinctively know when their organisation allows them to target someone and force them to feel uncomfortable, fearful and powerless. Oddly enough, although sociopaths enjoy destroying people, most people who use bullying behaviours don't consciously want to injure their target. Thus the behaviours experienced by the target as bullying are not necessarily perceived as bullying by the other person, who claims, 'I always shout and swear', 'She's just sensitive', or 'He's not doing his job properly'. This perception of innocence occurs despite the bully leaving a traumatic impact on the target, such as visible emotional scarring, or identifiable symptoms or injury. The ordinary bully wants to play games, pursue their career goals and eliminate potential threats and payback. Paradoxically, they would be horrified, humiliated and ashamed to be labelled a bully!

Workplace bullying is complex

Bullying may feel like a pinprick, a slow-growing cancer or a vicious assault. You can be bullied by one person or mobbed by a group. Some bullies select one target while others bully a number. Sometimes the real bully is disguised, so you only see their puppet. Some behaviours like bantering, teasing, screaming and exclusion occur regularly in your private life with family or friends and function as everyday work practices, whereas other behaviours are violent, abusive and criminal.

More recently, the hazards associated with cyber bullying at school are infiltrating the workplace, providing bullying around the clock. The subtle, passive-aggressive tone of an email, a poorly expressed communication, the requirement to have your mobile phone on night and day, the lack of inhibition online and the use of inappropriate material constitute an abuse of power. The absence of immediate feedback about its impact on the receiver means that the sender cannot see the damage online and remains unaware when they have hurt the receiver.

Duration

Although most workers will experience some isolated bullying behaviours across their life, the term 'bullying' is used when the behaviours occur over a period of time. The current baseline is about 6 months, and the average length of bullying is 15 months, although people can be bullied for more than 5 years. Beware that bullying can also include one incident that affects you every day; for example, removal of your work computer, a nasty piece on a website that is difficult to remove, a refusal to provide a correct phone headset.

Who can bully you?

Apart from saints who never abuse power, and sociopaths who instinctively abuse power, almost anyone can be targeted or use bullying behaviours, regardless of their career or position on the hierarchical ladder. Although there is limited research about bullies, it is clear that they come in all shapes, sizes and disguises. You can be bullied from all directions — by management, directors, clients, and customers. You can be bullied by your peers — *horizontal violence*; or by subordinates — *upwards bullying*, where employees peck away persistently at a manager to destroy them. Contractors bully permanent employees to get their job when the employ-

---

Are you a target?

- *Do you feel powerless, threatened, misused or abused at work?*
- *Could the person have dealt with you in a more respectful, effective manner?*
- *Would a videotape of cumulative behaviours be identified as bullying?*
- *Would other people regard the same behaviours as bullying if they were targeted?*
- *Would the person tolerate the same behaviours towards them?*
- *If it wasn't bullying, what was it?*

---

ment market is volatile. However, supervisors and managers bully more often because they find it easier to get away with it.

Are there gender variations?

> *The sisterhood betrays one another whereas the boys' club sticks together.*

Men and women seem to both bully, but as more managers are male, men do more bullying than women. In Europe, two in three targets are female. Although both sexes experience most forms of bullying, men experience more physical abuse and ganging up, whereas women experience more unfair criticism and sexual harassment.

Males use their aggressive, hunting instincts to confront, shout, frighten and humiliate. They roar like a bull, fight like a pit bull and exclude by using their boys' clubs or the 'glass ceiling'. Women are gatherers, who are socialised to be passive-aggressive. Thus female bullies devalue, exclude, or spread rumours about other women, attacking their target's self-esteem quietly until they strip something from them, or they copy aggressive male role models.

Some workplaces foster bullying

Although bullying can happen anywhere, research has shown that it appears to be more common in bureaucracies such as the public service, as well as the health sector (e.g., nursing, medicine, ambulance services), welfare (e.g., psychology, community care), education (schools and academia) and government-funded organisations. It is also common in

Animal quiz

Have you seen any of these creatures around the office lately?

Lion — constantly roaring throughout the workplace.

Saltwater crocodile — enjoys taking you into the death roll.

Wolf — charming to your face then attacks from behind.

Octopus — slowly engulfs you with aggression from all sides.

Giraffe — seems innocent, then leans in from afar to bully.

Peacock — so confident they don't care how their words or actions hurt.

Gorilla — only placated by subservient behaviours.

Shark — takes a bite out of you first and asks questions later.

Cat — scratches away but pretends to be righteous.

Grizzly bear — rears up and towers over you, ready to pounce.

Piranha — keeps chewing away until nothing's left.

Spider — invites you into their web and then destroys you.

Bee — attacks you when it perceives a threat to its hive.

manufacturing, retail, hospitality, call centres, and apprenticeships, or where there are high numbers of casual or contracted staff such as the arts, and those with a strong tradition of hierarchy, such as the law, army or police.

While the reason that some workplaces report higher incidents of bullying than others relates to poor management, in others it may be due to a better awareness of the need to report bullying.

Prevalence of bullying

We know that more than one in six children[7] are bullied weekly at school, and it seems that little changes when we grow up and enter the workforce. Based on a range of research, an average of 15–25% of employees report being bullied at work though it is higher in some organisations. Thus more people are bullied at work than at school![8] Although the type of bullying can vary according to culture, country, economy and industry, the actual prevalence is affected by cultural ways of defining bullying behaviours and the data selection process, such as incidence versus actual reporting. However, what is apparent is that often the target's perceptions are supported by witnesses who can identify the bullying and may also be injured by it.

The critical dilemma — beware of false labelling

Although the growing awareness of workplace bullying is constructive, it can foster misuse of the label 'target' or 'bully'. Unfortunately, bullying can be used as a weapon to attack employees and managers. Thus it is easier to blame an employee than to take responsibility for managerial and structural difficulties. Some employees claim victimisation to avoid accountability. Others will use bullying as payback for appropriate but unwelcome work practices. In one study of a large commercial office, half the managers were wrongly accused of being bullies.[9]

Do a gut check

Whenever I attend a social gathering or professional meeting or present a seminar, I chat about my interest in workplace bullying. Nearly every time, someone will give me a certain *look*. This look shows me that they understand exactly what I mean, and have a story based upon a personal, painful experience. Some of their stories are included in this book. Some would say, 'I'm not sure if this is making any sense', or 'I'm not sure if this is what you're looking for' and, despite my assurances of confidentiality, 'Please disguise identifying features'.

Many targets find it difficult to identify whether they are being bullied or not, which makes it harder to confront, so they become silenced by doubt and shame. Sadly, years later, many still feel this familiar sense of confusion and humiliation. Thus you need to do your own gut check and plan your action.

Obstacles to the prevention of workplace bullying

Perhaps the greatest handicap in the fight against workplace bullying is the lack of research. Currently, we are only seeing the tip of the bullying iceberg, thus knowledge about understanding and dealing with workplace bullying is in its infancy. This affects how it is identified, understood, confronted and prevented. Research and training are handicapped by a strange oxymoron; instead of accepting the high statistical probability of bullying occurring in any workplace, it generates extremely high levels of denial, fear and anger — bullying is a sensitive topic! Currently, there is no accepted international diagnosis for what I have termed *workplace bullying trauma*. Thus the medical, psychological, psychiatric and legal professions often disguise it as stress and adjustment disorders, without reference to actual symptoms. This undermines its severity, thereby sabotaging current understanding, treatment and rehabilitation. Following is a list of reasons why workplace bullying is so prevalent.

- Bullying as a concept is used to exploit employees, avoid organisational responsibility or is rationalised with labels such as 'leadership style'.
- Although some organisations systemically facilitate bullying, they regard it as a taboo subject, and no attempt is made to remedy the practice.
- Despite their legal obligations, employers pay lip-service to reducing bullying and its side effects.
- Organisations who fear legal liability deny its toxic damage. They are reluctant to publicly expose their dirty secrets. They may attempt to silence targets with confidentiality agreements or bully whistleblowers, and prevent researchers, investigators, insurance companies and media from assessing their internal structures.
- Organisations tend to solely blame targets and bullies instead of assuming responsibility for creating the professional incompetence that enabled the bullying.
- Targets feel ashamed, scared to share their stories and support one another. They fear retaliation by their employer or the bully, and are frightened that they will never be employed again if they speak out.
- There is limited acknowledgment of workplace bullying in textbooks — for example, in psychology or HR — and limited discussion at professional conferences that focus on management, leadership, HR, occupational health or psychology.
- Research is carried out under a range of descriptors, such as 'mobbing' or 'occupational violence', and across a number of professional areas, for example, in management, occupational health and safety, or psychology.

These aspects therefore limit the information about best practice procedures for organisations to collaborate with staff to support targets, rehabilitate bullies and develop a nontoxic workplace.

Bullying behaviours checklist[10]

Do you or someone else use these behaviours at work regularly?

- *Aggressive nonverbal behaviours* — scowling, snarling, staring, pointing, using subtle gestures (e.g., eye-rolling), physical intimidation, stalking, terrorising, criminal assault.

- *Abusive verbal behaviours* — teasing, taunting, ridiculing, using unacceptable nicknames, being rude or sarcastic, shouting, swearing, screaming.

- *Arrogance* — being impatient, interrupting, not listening, ignoring employees' opinions, lacking empathy, not perceiving distress.

- *Inadequate communication skills* — ignoring verbal and nonverbal feedback, unable to give instructions appropriately or provide constructive feedback.

- *Poor dispute resolutions skills* — avoiding requests for assistance, avoiding responsibility to collaborate and resolve conflicts.

- *Antisocial behaviours* — creating and controlling a toxic work culture, making employees feel powerless, enjoying employees' helplessness, fear, anger and tears.

- *Hypocrisy* — being nice to your face but nasty behind your back, flattering those with more power and bullying those with less, using convincing, compulsive lies.

- *Retaliation* — following constructive/courageous conversation or work-related feedback, imposing unwarranted disciplinary action or performance review, blackmail, extortion.

- *Threats* — giving offensive personal or professional comments that criticise, harass and humiliate, overtly/covertly, publicly or privately, to prevent speaking out; attempting to scapegoat the target, from jealousy, or concern the target may want their job, or fearing exposure for unethical behaviours and/or incompetencies.

- *Malicious rumours* — spreading personal or professional malicious gossip, verbally or with cyber/electronic tools such as email, text, social networking sites, where the target's complaints are treated as trivial or malicious.

- *Micromanagement* — excessive monitoring, constant criticism of trivial work matters, singling out one employee for review, or persecuting a person for minor mistakes everyone else makes regularly.

- *Sabotage* — preventing employees from fulfilling optimum job requirements by overloading them with work, manipulating relevant information, providing poor equipment, removing or hiding property/vital notes, altering or erasing computer files and settings, denying access to clients/information/facilities, collecting minor mistakes that are reframed as 'repeated failures' that the target cannot repudiate.

- *Abuse of justice* — treating some employees unfairly and unreasonably, such as blocking promotion, refusing requests for leave, reducing shifts or manipulating them, stealing credit for their work, restricting extra training, obtaining their job for a mate.

- *Distortion/misinformation* — manipulating other employees' perceptions by minimising achievements, exaggerating faults, stealing credit for their work, creating false impressions/accusations about their personality, mistakes, achievements and state of mind.

- *Exploitation* — imposing unreasonable, exploitative goals or deadlines with complicated work tasks or difficult shifts in order to achieve more or force them to fail.

- *Denigration* — removing former responsibilities and replacing them with trivial, unimportant chores or unpleasant tasks; negating the value of dispute resolution procedures, workplace bullying and harassment training sessions.

- *Discrimination* — harassing or excluding people on the basis of age, race, religion, culture, nationality, gender, sex, physical injury/handicap or psychological vulnerability from social or work-related events (e.g., meetings, emails, training).

- *Mobbing* — instructing other employees to disregard, exclude, abuse, spread rumours or cease contact with a target, or joining a mob to bully others.

- *Protection* — using compliant employees to build a support team and alienate nonsupporters.

Understanding workplace bullying

❝*I'm still at the same workplace where my toxic manager began in 1995. I began my 19th year there last month. In 1999, the company fired him, the day after he violently exploded at me in front of a half dozen witnesses (usually he bullied his targets in private). To a large extent the toxic environment still remains the same. Just different players or — more accurately, perhaps — a heightened awareness on my part, along with greater clarity now about how these 'other' players have in reality figured into the drama all along.*

From what I've read and studied extensively on this topic since 1996, I don't believe my own toxic workplace experience is atypical. Today I've learned to function very efficiently and pro-ductively in the midst of this tragic environment. I see clearly what's happening around me. I've developed good bound-aries, which effectively stave off bullying attempts by others. I remain aware, clear and centred, and most of the immature behaviour makes sense to me, within its own dysfunctional context. It saddens me deeply to see such a tragic waste of human resources, energy and talent. Where I can, I quietly validate and enlighten fellow colleagues in my workplace so they may empower and protect themselves. ❞

From bully bashing to victim blaming

Some years ago I went to a conference on workplace bullying in Queensland and discovered that if we eliminated bullies from the work-place, there wouldn't be many people left to work! Sometime later I spoke to a group of lawyers. The senior partner looked me straight in the eye and in front of all his colleagues informed me that he was a bully and even admitted to using bullying behaviours on his children.

The fact is, most people have experienced, witnessed, or used bullying behaviours. Parents and teachers bully occasionally, while siblings, close friends and workmates banter constantly. Nearly everyone has consciously and unconsciously bantered, teased, denigrated, harassed, sabotaged, excluded or bullied others at some stage. In fact, most people turn a blind eye to subtle bullying by family or friends, and ignore abusive bullying until it escalates and injuries occur, such as with domestic violence.

According to British psychologist and author Noreen Tehrani, sometimes it's hard to distinguish between who is bullying and who is being targeted; the target can bully and the bully can be victimised. Sometimes they become entwined in a macabre game by changing roles, and when targets try to protect themselves, bullies may even claim victimisation. Furthermore, bullies and targets are created and victimised by organisational systems — including employers, insurance companies, medico–legal professionals and industrial legislation — which blame and shame rather than build workplace collaboration. Thus it is pointless to simply attack bullies or blame victims.

Why does it happen?

Bullying can happen in any organisation, small or large, professional, commercial, public or trade. So far, the evidence is confusing and complex. Many factors can encourage bullying behaviours and maintain them such as the tribal cultures, individual personalities, work and social skills of target and bully; the actual work influences such as location, work culture, job stressors, quality of leadership skills, bystander behaviours, organisational structure and responses to bullying. In addition, all social behaviour, including bullying, can be affected by the economy, legislative changes, media, and the political climate.

When the employment world is tough, survival of the fittest, not the most competent, becomes the norm. Anyone working in a hostile environment should be ready to fight or flee to survive, even though this creates a less productive work culture. Many organisations create dysfunctional systems by allowing their boundaries or cultural systems to constantly change. Employees who do not know the rules of the game, or where the goalposts are located, can be oblivious to the onset of bullying and unable to protect themselves when they should. Like most other forms of abuse,

Have you experienced or used these bullying behaviours?

- teasing
- gossip
- nasty jokes
- verbal abuse
- denigration
- blame
- dirty looks
- sexual or gender harassment

- racial or religious denigration
- nasty notes
- public/private humiliation
- exclusion
- deception
- blackmail
- violence

bullying also thrives on secrecy and silence. It escalates because no-one confronts it and nothing effective is done to stop it when it is finally reported.

Although bullying can occur anywhere, when it occurs at work management is responsible for dealing with its consequences. Unfortunately, work complaints are often regarded as problems by management, although they should be interpreted as valuable feedback. Management may not realise that bullying represents incompetence and mismanagement, thus managers play adversarial games instead of focusing on their major goals. They don't have effective strategies to deal with bullying, so they employ antagonistic tactics instead of collaborative techniques, thereby exacerbating the situation. Unfortunately most organisations fail to respond quickly, effectively and respectfully when bullying occurs. Their denial of bullying behaviours, lack of responsibility and manipulation of the evidence further sabotages their employees and their company.

Tribal culture

Research shows that most people follow their tribe. A number of well-documented social experiments have clearly illustrated the development of strong 'us and them' feelings in ordinary people. In 1922, at Yale University, social psychologist Stanley Milgram wanted to discover how ordinary German citizens had come to commit the crimes of the holocaust. Under the guise of a study into the pain of learning, he paid volunteers to act as teachers. They were instructed by supervisors to give electric shocks when a student gave a wrong answer. The volunteer teachers followed the instructions and administered increasing shocks so intense as to reach the point at which the student would be unconscious and in danger of dying. The teachers didn't know that the equipment was fake, or that the students were actors. Milgram described the results as 'terrifying and depressing'. His 'obedience experiments' as they became known, showed that most ordinary people follow the leader. They sacrifice their moral values and empathy for others to obey their leader and survive with their tribe. Only 10% of Milgram's teachers refused instructions to continue shocking students who were clearly already distressed. Obedience to authority, as measured by a range of techniques, varies from country to country; it is higher in South Africa (80%) but lower in Australia (28%). (A recently replicated study in the United States by Jerry M. Burger[1] found only slightly lower rates 50 years later.)

In 1971 psychologist Philip Zimbardo conducted the famous 'Prison Experiment' at Stanford University using normal, postgraduate college students. They were divided into two groups; the mock guards quickly escalated from unkind behaviours to brutality, while their prisoners experienced severe emotional distress.[2] This experiment was terminated after 6 days because of the dramatic changes in personality and behaviours shown by the students. Zimbardo (2004)[3] describes evil as the exercise of power to harm, hurt, destroy and commit crimes against humanity:

> The line between good and evil is not fixed, it is permeable. Any one of us can move across it. We all have the capacity for love and evil — to be Mother Teresa, to be Hitler or Saddam Hussein. You don't need a motive, all you really need is a situation that facilitates moving across that line of good and evil.

Good people turn evil when they dehumanise their victim and project their responsibility onto others. They accept evil by doing nothing or accepting an ideology that justifies evil.

Thus the average nice person is affected by where they are, not who they are. Most human beings are social animals who follow their tribe. Like the members of a cult, few people have the courage to defy a tyrant. Thus employees behave with respect and empathy in a healthy workplace and become offensive or defensive in a dysfunctional one. Then anyone can be targeted or bully, the climate can change, compliance becomes compulsory, dictators are created and emulated, and minor negative behaviours escalate into major harm.

The work tribe bullies out employees whom they believe don't fit with their culture or threaten it. A minor ritual, like exclusion from the lunch table, reduces status and represents tribal disapproval. Most people have a primitive survival fear of being rejected by their tribe, thus they feel obliged to do what is necessary to belong to it.

If you want to belong to a tribe you must accept its pecking order. The pack instinct herds you into valuing the tribal leaders who guide and protect you, so you model their behaviours. Although no-one likes a bully, if your leader is a bully you use defence mechanisms such as denial to pretend they are normal. Much like the emperor with no clothes, you choose to believe they are no different. You flatter those with more power and denigrate those with less. It's easier to follow the tribe than stand up for justice. Besides, if you challenge the status quo you also risk being bullied.

Who uses bullying behaviours?

'For years my bullying behaviours were acceptable. Suddenly the government decides it's not OK for me to yell, so I become a test case, denigrated, undermined, intimidated.'

There are a variety of bullies. The aggressive bully who screams, threatens and blames is easily noticed, whereas the passive-aggressive bully who divides and conquers is camouflaged and extremely difficult to identify. Likewise the 'good cop/bad cop' game where one bully is 'nice' while another does his dirty work; or the two-faced bully who flatters important clients and senior management but bullies those lower down, are confusing. Other bullies present a caring facade, but reveal contempt when compassion is required, or turn against someone who was caring towards them. Some bullies aim everywhere, others select their targets, and some targets have one bully, while others experience mobbing by a number of bullies.

The main types of bullies

The bullies you may have met at school also go to work. They include the malicious or serial bully, the nonmalicious bully and the provocative bully/target. Most bullies are ordinary people who use a mixture of bullying behaviours to achieve their goals, avoid confrontation or survive at work. They don't realise that their toxic patterns of behaving are

harmful and humiliating, nor do they consciously wish to hurt others. They can experience real distress when confronted. However, most bullies intuitively identify when their employer and managers encourage, silently condone or passively enable them to bully.

A simple classification system of bullies

I use metaphors to classify bullies into two main groups, the saltwater crocodile (the *sociopathic bully*) and the fowls that play foul (the *ordinary bully*). These are obviously *not* clinical descriptions; just *empowering* ones to help victims plan their action.

Type 1: The saltwater crocodile

> *The saltwater crocodile's mission is to protect his family and territory. He studies your patterns of behaviour and then uses cunning to stalk a vulnerable being and attack. Once he grabs the struggling victim, he thrusts them into the death roll. He's less interested in cold, inanimate animals. When a crocodile escapes, he changes his strategies to avoid capture. The moral is to be unpredictable. Change your behaviours or he will work out your vulnerabilities.*

Common descriptions: Queen Bee, boss bitch, bully broad, boss from hell, ice queen, sociopath in a suit, terminator, social terrorist, 'Dr Jekyll and Mr Hyde', social predator, pit bull, dominatrix.

Clinical descriptions include: antisocial personality disorder, sociopath, psychopath, narcissistic personality disorder, paranoid personality disorder, borderline personality disorder.

The saltwater crocodile has an internal coldness, cunning and callousness, while externally being hypocritical, deceitful, pathological liars. They can appear caring and superficially charming while internally they are arrogant and lack empathy. They love power and therefore they control, dominate or manipulate people for their own needs, taking what they want and doing as they please, violating social norms and expectations without guilt or remorse. As long as they get what they want, they don't care if they hurt, intimidate or abuse others. These social predators are natural bullies.

- The sociopath or psychopath[4] has genetic brain abnormalities that make them think, feel and relate differently.
- They don't process intellectual or emotional material like the average person.
- They sweat less and show less distress when threatened.
- Unlike normal people, they lack remorse, guilt or empathy for their victims.
- They can't accept responsibility for their actions.
- You may get a gut feeling that they're different.
- Statistically, about 4% of the population has an antisocial disorder (3% males and 1% females), including 1% who are psychopaths.

Although the *saltwater crocodile* at work is as egocentric, callous and manipulative as the average criminal psychopath, they use their intelligence, family background, social skills and circumstances to construct a facade of normalcy to get what they want, without landing in jail. They're attracted to the bright lights and action (e.g., politics, law enforcement, military) or to workplaces with a belief in the natural goodness of others, where it's easier to abuse or defraud others. According to psychologist Robert Hare,[5] whose research centred on psychopathology and psychophysiology, corporate psychopaths score high on his psychopathy checklist for the remorseless use of others and their enjoyment in hurting them. People believe their superficial charm and qualifications, without identifying the evil, predatorial game behind the facade. They're cool under pressure, love the thrill of chaos, upheaval and change (e.g., downsizing and mergers), which hides their abusive behaviours. While they tread over bodies for higher profits, the actual long-term net results can be far less. Meanwhile, their games disguise their personal and professional weaknesses. Their huge egos, short tempers and need for excitement create a dangerous organisational cocktail.

Type 2: The fowls who play foul

'Julie is a strong manager, she kicks arse.'

Some people are born more aggressive, others are conditioned to become abusive, but most people use bullying behaviours to survive and thrive. These fowls play foul to feather their nest and follow the crowd. Some regard their behaviours as meaningless or harmless, they often rationalise their use — to get the job done or to build their power base. Thus the arrogant, egocentric bullies whose political power or expertise appears to make megabucks for their company (before a comprehensive financial audit) believe their bullying makes them successful or regard it as an essential component of their company's culture.

Others are unaware, under extreme pressure or have poor management skills. They project their feeling of powerlessness onto those they can bully and avoid those they can't. Some use skills they have developed over years to survive, because they don't know how to communicate assertively, like the woman with the seductive, measured, manipulative voice or the man who says, 'Just do it!'

There is far less research about the ordinary bully; they are not investigated like psychopaths and antisocial personality disorders or referred for personality or psychiatric assessments like their targets. Ultimately, they can be nearly anyone. Here are some simple examples:

The peacock. The peacock is a beautiful, noisy ornamental bird. The male peacock shows off its magnificent feathers while courting the plainer peahen. They roam around with a cry that sounds like 'help'.

These bullies don't mean to aggravate or hurt, they're just having fun or doing their job. They strut around and fluff out their ego like feathers.

In Australia, from footballers to surgeons, they're known as *fig jam* (*Fuck I'm good, just ask me*).

They say, 'We're just having fun', 'I got the better of him', 'You're not as good as us', 'You're different to us', 'That's the way we do things here', 'It's all part of getting ahead', 'If you can't take the heat get out of the kitchen', 'I'm the king of the castle and you're the dirty rascal'.

The lyrebird. The lyrebird learns from older lyrebirds and can mimic almost any sound with great accuracy including other birds, chainsaws and rifle shots. They're well disguised in their habitat, and although they make the right noises, when you need them they are hard to find.

This bully has an insecure, manipulative personality and fears threats and bullying. She needs to survive at work and goes with the flow, so like a chameleon she copies the role models around her. She appears supportive and says, 'Go get them', but then sabotages you by saying, 'I can't give you a witness statement now because I might lose my job'. Although you were good friends for years and perhaps you helped her out or exchanged birthday cards, she abandons you in court when things get tough.

The barnyard fowl. Chickens are less aggressive in the clear boundaries of a pen. The hierarchical pecking order disintegrates in the large, open, free-range environments. Strange chicken encounters occur. Aggressive chickens peck away at the weaker chickens until they die. It's survival of the fittest.

This type of bully believes that it is acceptable to attack when everyone else does. They join the mob to belong and prevent themselves from being bullied. They pick on someone who is vulnerable and peck away until they're destroyed. They forget previous friendships, past loyalties and personal ethics to destroy a former mate. These bullies are constantly nitpicking, do minimal work and exclude those who're different.

The bully–target nexus

> *'The woman doctor leaned across to me during the concert and shouted in my ear, "Will you stop chewing loudly". Though the content was appropriate, her message was poorly relayed. I spent much of the concert planning how to retaliate for her rudeness. I wonder if that is how bullying begins?'*

> *'The mining truck drivers are highly paid, their job is easy and there's little competition. Some of them bully their managers to avoid extra work, so their managers react.'*

> *'Nellie is proud of her ability to survive in the difficult world of work. When she's challenged, instead of sucking up, blocking or humouring, she questions and attacks back. She changes the game from banter to bullying.'*

Just like schoolyard bullying, workplace bullying can become a provocative, reciprocated game where both parties are targeted or bully. If a target or manager reports bullying they can be sabotaged by superficial, adversarial policies, handicapped by lack of senior management support and manipulated by the HR people who support senior management and who in turn have been bullied. The game is exacerbated, and the wrong person can be accused and punished.

Some bullies are oblivious to the impact of their bullying behaviours on their target because they don't identify the negative reactions from the victim. Simultaneously, some targets don't know how to block the bullying and disguise their reaction.

A target's perception of a bullying event may also aggravate an initial minor altercation into a larger ongoing problem.

Some targets exacerbate a bullying situation by waiting for months instead of acting immediately after the bullying occurs. Consequently, when the frustrated target finally confronts their bully, their pent-up feelings change their response into an attack, and the bully feels threatened and reacts.

The bullying game

It is important to understand that the bullying process at work is not a single, solitary incident, performance review or disciplinary action. It is different to the danger associated with faulty machinery or stressful work projects. The bully needs a target or scapegoat, and the victim is in the wrong place at the wrong time. Generally, the victim did not provoke the bully, although they may have threatened him when they questioned, confronted or disputed something (e.g., a request for equal shifts or a work problem).

The bully begins his attack in a simple, subtle, gradual way, such as bantering, to undermine the target, followed by indirect bullying behaviours; for example, removing secretarial help, or shifting the target to a worse office. The bully senses powerlessness. Once a target reacts and stands up for themself, the bully feels justifiably provoked. He retaliates and the conflict grows.

The bully game becomes more overt and aggressive as the bully builds his social links with colleagues. He may use past experiences to protect himself and create a culture of fear or, alternatively, use a culture of ignorance to stop everyone supporting the target. He manipulates management with his malicious rumours, so they turn against the target. Although everyone makes mistakes, the bully manager uses minor ones, often from long ago, to build a case. He slowly reduces the target's ability to defend or protect themself. If the target makes a genuine mistake because of high stress levels and associated reduced concentration, the bully challenges their professional integrity.

This common problem (the game) escalates until everyone turns either against the target or moves away from the conflict and avoids getting involved. The target becomes socially isolated, publicly humiliated and stigmatised. Their self-esteem deteriorates, stress and frustration increase, and motivation is reduced. The bully may use more physical, verbal and psychological violence to victimise the target further (e.g., shove them out of his way). The target's physical and mental health continues to deteriorate, and they are forced to move, resign or be dismissed.

Meanwhile, the employers who are too frightened of confronting the bully may promote them out of an area or provide them with an excellent reference to move on, where they continue to bully.

Bullying tactics

> *Talia knew that Mick was nasty — 'If I didn't play up to him he'd get me' — while believing that Jim, his boss, was decent — until she discovered that Jim denigrated staff, sacked his faithful secretary of 15 years, fiddled the books, and supported another bully. Talia knew it was risky to challenge Mick, but she hadn't identified Jim's true colours, as a peacock. She was unaware of the damage Jim had done until he denied her insurance claim and she wasn't paid until months later, following legal action. She was hurt, shocked and angry that he turned against her.*
>
> *John, the actual bully, is nice to Ann (especially after setting her up), and says nice things about her to HR but sabotages behind her back. When Ann complains, HR says, 'But he says nice things about you!'*

Bullies know how to *walk the walk* and *talk the talk*. They're extremely good at promoting themselves by using charm and mind games to influence, manipulate and control others. Many bullies create a gang to support their climb up the status ladder, while their cronies hang onto their coattails for security, rank or promotion. Their power comes from covert psychological manipulation or overt aggression. They know when their actions are sanctioned by their employer and will manoeuvre others to remain silent, knowing that when careers are under threat other employees won't take action and so remain detached to avoid being targeted next. Thus bullying is facilitated by a cultural code of silence, caused by conditioning, habit, fear or 'schadenfreude' (*pleasure at someone else's misfortune*).

People only know what the bully wants them to know, so bullies show managers their charming facade, but expose their malicious self to targets. They distort reality using a combination of withholding information and spreading misinformation. Their political games portray the target as a bad performer to undermine them, and prove their assertion by finding a minor problem to repudiate the target's reputation. Unfortunately, when bullying is disguised it is harder to disprove their allegations and so a request for help is more likely to be rejected.

The bully may manipulate witnesses to mob a target, while providing them with support and sympathy. Although witnesses can suffer directly or indirectly from the bullying, they don't always understand the bully's toxic games. They may see some trivial, subtle bullying incidents without identifying the bigger picture. Witnesses may bitch to one another, but few confront the bully or complain to someone responsible.

While bullying sometimes goes on behind closed doors, nevertheless bullies make sure that others know. This warns whistleblowers to be quiet, reinforces the bully's power, and condemns the target. When people are scared they don't know what to do, so they do nothing, which enables the bullying to escalate. Few people have the courage to stand up to the bully; instead they make excuses and say *That's business*. Anyone who feels threatened or tired of the victim's complaints joins the mob to attack.

Bullies are extremely vindictive and self-protective. They will attempt to destroy anyone who sees through their nasty games. Once a target is too injured to work and is forced to leave, bullies or their managers will try to forbid any contact with the target, in case the target gives a truer version of events or the cause of their workplace injuries are identified.

Serial bullies

> *'I worked for a psychopath boss for 14 years. Due to my international reputation, I was asked to speak overseas, but he went instead and at other times he would give me a week's notice to travel. On one occasion I was scared the stress would kill me. He's very subtle, shrewd and cunning and catches the junior staff off balance, affecting more than 30 employees. He's got degrees in everything except emotional intelligence. His own standard of work is below par, and he is destroying the name of our department. Human resources are powerless and claim he's untouchable. We have crocodile-free days when he's not at work.'*

The serial bully[6] swings through a workplace like a wrecking ball on a demolition site. They're programmed to take live targets and destroy them. They will bully any time and any place. This social predator establishes his power by creating support for himself throughout the company. He divides employees into those who support or flatter and those who challenge him. Once established, he targets those who threaten him. He turns work colleagues and superiors against the target, so they deny the target's complaints and blame them. Eventually he destroys their career and reputation. Sometimes he eliminates other threats by destroying his mentors and assuming control.

Serial bullies fear exposure. When confronted, they use a variety of tactics, including denial, avoidance and blame. Once he eliminates one target, he waits until everything settles down, then selects another target to isolate, disable and annihilate. This cycle continues until the bully leaves.

From one workplace to the next, they leave a trail of destruction, solely focused on fulfilling their own paranoid need for power. Their bullying behaviours are unrelated to the goals and ambitions of their organisation.

Understanding the bully's perspective

A person who works alone can't bully, whereas an employee whose work depends upon collaborating with other staff can.

A target's pain is a bully's gain

> *Anita's boss is known as a bully around the hospital. He was bullied at school and enjoys subtle power games. He's really nice to senior doctors, but bullies peers and subordinates. He picks*

on different people, without reason, for small, unpredictable things for a few weeks. It's scarier to be in his good books because you don't know when he will turn. He describes his style as a benign dictatorship. Although it's possible to guess the next target, usually those weaker, sometimes he targets the strong. In the past 4 years, eight people have left because of his bullying.

At some primitive level, just like an animal, bullies recognise when their targets are feeling uncomfortable, insecure or threatened. Paradoxically, this is exactly what most bullies feel inside but deny. Although they're feeling frightened and out of control internally, they project their fears, frustrations and powerlessness onto others. A bully forces their target into survival mode. When the target shows their fight or flight feelings in a passive or aggressive manner, they lose control and donate power to the bully. This makes the bully happy. They can focus on the target's discomfort and powerlessness, not their own.

Why do bullies bully?

'Nobody stops me.'

'I need to survive.'

'I can get away with it.'

'I'm the one being bullied.'

'We enjoy eliminating people who're different.'

'The boss sees me taking action.'

'Workplaces aren't kindergartens.'

'It's the survival of the fittest in this jungle.'

'That's how we operate here.'

'We need to camouflage incompetence, mismanagement or fraud.'

'It's just a bit of fun.'

'I've always related to staff this way.'

'I can't see what the fuss is about, this is life.'

'It doesn't matter how I say it, you still have to do it.'

Bullying behaviours are learned

Most bullies begin their apprenticeship at home, witnessing aggression and helplessness and experimenting in the sandpit. Then they graduate from school and practise their craft in the workplace. Most school bullies receive limited love, inconsistent guidelines, inappropriate role models or abuse at home. Their behaviours are reinforced by inadequate school systems. Their skills of empathy, self-control, and ability to tolerate frustration are limited. They lack effective communication skills so they fight or manipulate to survive. They learn passive and aggressive behaviours by copying others and no-one makes them accountable, in fact some feel rewarded. Sometimes ex-school targets can undergo a metamorphosis by transforming themselves into workplace bullies; their motto is, *if you can't beat them, join them.* Those who were provocative at school continue to be so at work.

Although anyone can use bullying behaviours, bullies thrive in dysfunctional, adversarial systems. The longer the bullying occurs, the more people can become involved. Other targets and onlookers get worn down over time, confronting or avoiding the bullying. Like animals, the pack follows the bully leader to survive.

Laura Crawshaw,[7] founder of Executive Insight, an organisation that has coached leaders in over 40 Fortune 500 companies throughout the world, notes that bullies are deficient in empathising — the ability to read other's behaviour — which is practised by all social animals, and necessary for detecting and responding to threats in the environment, as well as forming social bonds. Both employees and managers whose early family experiences lack a focus on feelings need coaching to minimise their abrasive behaviour.

Piranhas in the goldfish bowl

Bullies bully because they can. There are many reasons why employees get away with using bullying behaviours. An employer can create the work culture that allows bullying to survive. Like piranhas in the goldfish bowl, the scramble for individual power and status within a large company distorts value systems and corrupts work cultures. Arrogant employers can't see that bullying is a problem, or believe that their policies are adequate. They undervalue employees, enable corruption, dishonesty and unethical work practices. Adversarial employers choose win–lose battles, not collaborative win–win games.

Poorly trained managers with faulty beliefs, values and attitudes can foster bullying behaviours. Scapegoating makes an incompetent manager appear proactive. Sometimes employees are sandwiched between a corporate bullying culture in the boardroom and a combative, bullying aggression by unions. Ultimately, the major cause of bullying at work is a workplace that overtly, covertly and subversively allows it.

Why is workplace bullying poorly understood?

Although occupational stress has interested academics and health practitioners for decades, understanding and dealing with bullying, violence and trauma at work is still a relatively new concept.

The far more researched area of school bullying has a wealth of research. Professor Dan Olweus has been involved in research and intervention work in the area of bully/victim problems among schoolchildren and youth in Norway for approximately 30 years. Since then, researchers have demonstrated its toxic nature to targets, bullies, parents and schools. Nowadays, education and psychology experts are developing effective theories and practical interventions to reduce school bullying. Schools are slowly acknowledging their legal and ethical responsibilities.

However, school bullying is far less complex than workplace bullying. It is more transparent and less devious. Most school targets intuitively understand that poor social-survival skills can trigger bullying. In contrast, adult targets of workplace bullying generally seem socially successful, competent, loyal employees who can't understand why it happened. They obtain less support, and their complaint is less likely to be acknowledged or validated.

Although school bullying and workplace bullying appear different, there are many similarities, including some injuries, treatment and the need for organisational restructuring. As research into workplace bullying is recent and restricted, our current knowledge, research and practical experience in dealing with school bullying is far more developed, thus the knowledge gained from school bullying is paving the way for understanding and dealing with workplace bullying.[8]

Workplace bullying researchers

In 1945, industrial psychologist C.A. Oakley[9] first described managers who bully, bluster and blame, and talked of the harm caused by workplace

BULLY BLOCKING AT WORK: A Self-Help Guide for Employees and Managers bullying. In 1976 the psychiatrist Caroll Brodsky[10] emphasised that bullying can only exist in a culture that permits it. The organisational psychologist Heinz Leymann pioneered research into group bullying or mobbing in the mid-1980s in Sweden, and he established a unique clinic at Violen for individuals traumatised by the workplace. The introduction of *The European Journal of Work and Organizational Psychology* legitimised the science of workplace bullying and mobbing. Other researchers at that time included Stale Einarsen (University of Bergen) and Helge Hoel (University of Manchester). In the early 1990s broadcaster and journalist Andrea Adams publicised the significance of workplace bullying in the United Kingdom. More recently, Professor of Human Resource Management at Portsmouth Business School, Charlotte Rayner, has written extensively on the topic of bullying at work. Other experts in this field include organisational counselling psychologist Noreen Tehrani and Professor of Mental Health and Youth at University of Surrey, Helen Cowie. Australian research began in the early 1990s with Paul McCarthy, Michael Sheehan and Michelle Barker from Griffith University, and the Beyond Bullying Association. In the United States, Ruth and Gary Namie, founders of the Workplace Bullying Institute, David Yamada, Director of the New Workplace Institute (www.newworkplaceinstitute.org) at Suffolk University Law School in Boston, social scientist Loraleigh Keashley and employee advocate Pamela Lutgen-Sandvik, are all active in researching bullying in the workplace. Many other people are currently researching the toxic nature of workplace bullying, including victims, unions, mental health professionals, journalists, women's organisations and government departments. Further awareness is promoted through their books, conferences, self-help groups and websites.[11] Sadly though, many activists, researchers and professionals in the area of workplace bullying have sacrificed their health, wellbeing and financial security through their efforts, becoming ill, burnt-out or even dying early.

While workplace bullying research is still a very recent area of study, there is growing organisational awareness about the economic benefits of treating employees with respect, reducing legal liability, and organisational development programs that focus upon improving the quality of leadership practices and organisational climate. Australian psychologists Peter Cotton and Peter Hart[12] note that these are likely to have a greater impact on reducing workers compensation premiums than traditional occupational health and safety risk-management approaches.

Current awareness

The first legislation dealing with bullying at work occurred in Sweden in 1993 and focused on organisational responsibilities, not individual issues. Although this legislation has been repealed, it has since been incorporated into broader legislation. The European Parliament emphasises the social corporate responsibility of employers. Some countries have developed guidelines or legislation to reduce physical bullying, sexual and racial harassment and workplace bullying. Hopefully, legislation will increase as people become increasingly aware of this toxic, dangerous, expensive phenomenon.

Conditions that encourage workplace bullying

> ❝The doctor used charm, confidence and cunning to establish his reputation at the hospital, and two neighbours described him as a nice fellow. He entertained medical staff lavishly, bought pizzas for theatre nurses, and expensive perfume for secretaries. While he conned hospital executives, who relished his profit producing operations, he didn't fool the head intensive-care nurse. When she challenged his medical incompetence, he bullied her. Her colleagues were too scared to support her request for an independent audit and the hospital filed her complaints away. She approached other hospital officials, the State Coroner, the Medical Board, police and Parliament. She was bullied, intimidated, threatened with disciplinary action, prosecution and sacking. ❞

The research to date identifies four major reasons[1] why bullying occurs in organisations:

1. unproductive working conditions
2. poor leadership
3. the target is different
4. poor ethical standards.

Condition 1: Unproductive working conditions

Poor working conditions lead to bullying because employees may become frustrated when they cannot do their work properly, or when work requirements are inappropriate or unfair, such as unequal shifts. In addition, restructuring, redundancy and fear reduce the number of mature, experienced employees who can mentor or support others.

Stressful physical working conditions

I once worked with a client who told me about a plastic surgeon who was raking in millions making patients look better while his stressed staff worked in cramped conditions because he was too mean to put on extra staff or make the offices attractive. Their obvious resentment to management was fertile ground for a bully. The design, structure, degree of isolation or physical layout of the workplace can be physically and psychologically dysfunctional and lead to worker distress. Working in noisy, hot, cold or cramped conditions is extremely stressful. Employees are also more likely to be bullied when office doors are closed, senior executives are cloistered away in their plush suites, and there are fewer witnesses. In contrast, the open plan office allows all behaviours to be witnessed, although this may also create a breeding ground for mobbing.

Old boy networks

> During the early 1990s Dr Stephen Bolsin was persistently ignored, ridiculed, harassed when he alerted British medical authorities about the alarming death rate among infants at a leading Bristol hospital. While highlighting the incompetence of two surgeons, he broke the unspoken rule — doctors don't dob on colleagues!

Belonging to the *old boys' club* is often the key to success. Board members are selected by peers and reflect their level of skills and cultural background, and they guard their territory. Nepotism replaces job interviews and sabotages performance reviews. Although a few women and atypical men break through the glass ceiling to challenge prevailing boardroom cultures, these are token changes in most parts of the world.

Old boy networks are prone to the use of bullying traditions that originate from their school days. From the privileged private school boys' club to the male stronghold of unions, the domino effect enables bullying traditions to survive. Members feel threatened by those who are different, and bully to protect their network, while the employee who doesn't belong is sandwiched in between. Bullying is perpetuated in boardrooms around the world and provides a template for the remainder of the organisation. Sadly, old boy networks consist of basically decent people, oblivious to the tribal behaviours that cause untold damage.

Women's business

> *Information is withheld; secrets are kept; a victim's contributions — to either a conversation or a workplace — are ignored.*[2]

While men respect their hunting partners and support them without judgment when threatened, some women appear to abandon their female colleagues. These gatherers are two-faced, passively turning against one another to survive. The small groups they use for socialising become a social weapon to exclude, isolate, ostracise and humiliate other women when under threat. They bully in subtle, passive, underhand ways, which go unnoticed by males who are more accustomed to identifying the more open and aggressive forms of bullying or abuse. This makes it harder to challenge and prove. Most women know it happens, they observe the damage it inflicts but are too scared to confront it.

Flawed workplace support structures

> *'The care factor is zero at present.'*

> *'I call them the Department of Hideous Services, not Human Services. All they do is cover their backside.'*

Old-style personnel departments were established to deal with employee welfare. Today's HR departments seem to have subtly shifted from a welfare emphasis to a problem-management emphasis. Thus while employees receive debriefing when they confront a violent critical incident such as a hold-up, many HR departments cannot identify or manage ongoing workplace bullying appropriately. They are forced to align their loyalty with their employer, not the employees, and appear under pressure to treat employees as disposable, instead of valuing them as a long-term resource. They don't seem to have enough knowledge or power to assist targets, bullies and others to improve their performance. They hide their conflict of interest as they use adversarial procedures to resolve disputes or promote and demote unfairly. They have a blind spot about auditing the high costs for their employer created by faulty management of workplace bullying.

Poor computer and internet use policies

The internet has grown like a huge, nuclear mushroom cloud. Although it has created a wonderful exciting world of connection and information, it is also being used as a weapon of mass destruction that can ruin a person's reputation, safety, health, wellbeing and social skills. Schools are rife with tales of cyber abuse, which adults are quickly copying. These include rude text messages, nasty visual images, and malicious postings on social networking sites like Facebook. Internet tools that can be so productive at work can also be misused to abuse employees and employers. Workplaces without clear computer and internet use guidelines are susceptible to the use of these work tools to facilitate bullying.

Lack of legal support

> *I have legal rights, but when estimating the costs I realised I could have lost my home, superannuation and everything! So where is justice and my legal rights?*

The fantasy world of the television courtroom persuades us that the law provides validation, justice, compensation and retribution. If you believe in justice, be aware that few bullying targets get a fair go. In many countries the more overt forms of bullying such as threats of violence, stalking, sexual harassment and racial discrimination are covered by legislation; by contrast, subtler forms of bullying such as denigrating, excluding or sabotaging work performance escape most codes of conduct and legislation.

Despite some changes in the law (e.g., equal opportunity, occupational health and safety) many bullying behaviours are still condoned or ignored. Though some countries have an automatic compensation system, in most countries organisations fear litigation, and try to sabotage justice and influence lawmakers. There are huge gaps between your experience of bullying, the action your organisation is legally compelled to take, your state or country's guidelines or statutory definitions, and the effectiveness of their legal implementation when you require justice.

Unfortunately most grievance procedures, such as mediation, can have an uncertain outcome. The high financial and psychological costs of legal assistance limit the number of victims who can access justice and increase disciplinary payouts. Therefore, the repercussions for breaking the law cause minimal consequences for large corporations. They are more likely to alter their bullying culture following the negative impact of union strikes, destructive publicity, increased legal fees and insurance costs.

Ineffective or negative worker union support

> Bill was the 11th manager in nine years for a large shipping corporation. The union bullied his predecessors out by vandalising their homes and gardens, writing 'Scab' everywhere. They were stalked, their phones were tapped and they received phone calls late at night.

Unions are an essential link in a worker's safety chain. They can assist members to deal with bullying by providing information and support; for example, writing letters, organising or attending meetings. They may investigate following a complaint, subsidise legal advice, initiate legal action, strike, sponsor research and promote awareness campaigns. However, union representatives can be bullied by employers to forgo their responsibilities, while others have limited intervention resources and lack the power to help their members. Sadly, unions can also create their own culture of bullying by forcing workers to join the union or support their style of working. Those who challenge unethical practices within the union can be ostracised, abused, allocated the worst jobs and problematic machinery, and live in fear for their lives. Their quest for political power and financial support can distort their values and members' prospects.

Condition 2: Poor leadership

Like the conductor of an orchestra, a manager leads his team to achieve specific work outcomes and deal with change, conflict and equity. If he lacks leadership skills, is arrogant, autocratic, passive, or scared of confrontation, he enables bullying. Sadly, many knowledgeable employees and professionals are promoted to managerial positions without any expectation of additional expertise in management skills and without any supervision, accountability, mentoring or training in these skills.

Lack of management skills

> 'In our workplace it was build up, burn up and bully out.'

Managers are appointed because of their professional expertise, self-promotional abilities or social networking skills. Good managers are assertive and communicate effectively, they confront change and other difficulties by mentoring, early intervention, resolving conflicts and providing constructive feedback.

Research indicates that many managers cannot identify inappropriate, unethical or bullying behaviours. They may seem like decent people, but when their management skills are poor or they lack managerial experience, they may become overcontrolling and manipulative, aggressive and humiliating if threatened. They bully instead of motivating, or become passive and allow others to bully instead. Thus bullying is often a smokescreen for personal or professional weaknesses and difficulties. Managers are more likely to project their poor people skills and powerlessness onto competent employees who challenge them than to target incompetent employees who crumble. Thus bullying is a sign of poor management and incompetence.

Empowerment vs. overpowerment

> Sam described his CEO as tough and hard. He had high expectations of all staff and fired anyone who made terrible mistakes. At the same time he was a nice human being, who encouraged his staff. When annoyed, he confronted openly, his criticism was justified, but he wasn't a bully!

Every child respects the parent or teacher who sets clear boundaries and fair consequences. In sport there is a clear difference between physical assertiveness and brutality. Similarly, there is a clear line between managers who use tough management practices and those who bully. However, much of the insecure corporate world seems to believe that profit is based on human sacrifice rather than collaboration. Success requires a psychological whip and comes at someone else's expense. Organisations with dysfunctional belief systems about the use of power encourage bullying rather than empowering their managers and employers.

Inability to deal with change

In the past few decades the average workplace has been overwhelmed with organisational restructures designed to enhance productivity. Companies are forced to meet tight financial goals while coping with budget restrictions. The private sector has the flexibility to adapt products and adjust prices to make a profit, whereas the public sector — such as health, education and welfare — have less flexibility but still face pressure to reduce costs. Management are forced to use incentives such as higher salary based on improved performance, or disincentives such as forcing employees to achieve more or face penalties or loss of entitlements. Organisational restructuring creates a heavier workload, micromanagement and constant leadership changes.

Bullying is often a byproduct of poor change-management strategies. Stressed managers blame people, not organisational factors. Targets make excellent scapegoats, especially when unstable job markets lower their opportunities to challenge bullying. The manager who eliminates the problem target is called proactive. In reality, whatever their excuse, bully managers damage morale, motivation, work performance and loyalty, with the result that the desired financial benefits of restructuring cannot be achieved.[3]

Poor conflict management

> 'As a professional who works in Learning and Development I am constantly amazed at how individuals in the work environment in particular don't handle conflict well and avoid confrontation, even with performance management. One of the main reasons given for people leaving their workplace is their manager! This will change only if the fear of confrontation is less than the fear of the outcome if one doesn't confront the issue.'

Like a family, employees continually confront differences of opinion, which can trigger constructive or destructive conflict. Good managers rely upon teamwork. When a disagreement requires a resolution, like responsible parents, they use collaborative procedures to resolve the complaint and move on.

However, poor leaders in dysfunctional organisations employ low levels of cooperation. A complaint may be regarded as threatening and denied, especially when litigation looms. When they camouflage a complaint or conflict, stress and abuse escalate, undermining staff morale and productivity so that eventually the situation explodes. Alternatively, employers overreact and use a bulldozer approach, when pliers would have been more effective in resolving the conflict. They launch a huge public investigation instead of a simple private discussion. Some managers will even collude with the bully and accept their biased perceptions. They protect, promote or export their bullies with good references, while simultaneously humiliating, disciplining and destroying their targets.

A number of common statements can be identified that are used by managers to avoid responsibility for workplace conflict that has spun out of control. These statements are made without proper investigation of all the evidence or any attempt to resolve individual differences using mentoring and/or restorative practices. Any mistake is used as an indelible example of the target's faults in every other area, without any reference to the mistakes and faults of everyone else in their department. Personality diagnoses are inappropriately thrown around like confetti, towards the target, nobody else. Examples include:

- The target's credibility can be attacked by statements such as 'That's the way we do things here' or 'They're too thin-skinned'.

- The causes of the conflict are relabelled as communication difficulties, a bad attitude, or 'It's a disciplinary/performance issue'.

Inadequate responses to bullying

> *'I'd rather work for the Mafia where the rules of the game are explicit, than work for a company that has a policy in name only. I thought they would take action, so I didn't protect myself.'*

There are usually many occasions when a manager could intervene and support a target from the moment bullying is detected. However, many won't because they don't understand what workplace bullying actually involves, its level of toxicity and what it takes to stop it. They may also believe their company's policies and procedures will deal with the problem effectively. That isn't always the case.

According to psychologist Pat Ferris,[4] there are three types of responses to bullying:

- See no evil. Bullying is considered normal, so targets must toughen up. Targets understand and are more likely to leave before they are seriously injured.
- Hear no evil. The organisation doesn't really care about bullying, their anti-bullying policies are deceptive and their interventions fail. This is common in hierarchical, not-for-profit or public service organisations. Targets are seriously injured, require longer therapy and are more likely to undertake protracted legal action.
- Speak no evil. Managers acknowledge bullying is harmful and follow organisational procedures that demonstrate respect for all employees, a view commonly found in private organisations. They resolve conflict and obtain help for those affected.

Organisational board blindness

> 'I told the seminar that the chief executive of a large corporation boasted how well his company dealt with bullying. Then a participant told me that she'd left a branch of his organisation because of the bullying!'

> The law firm advertises that it assists victims of bullying. Now it faces legal action by some of their staff who were bullied by one of their lawyers.

Most large public companies are directed by board members whose main focus is on the company's share price and public profile. Unfortunately, many demonstrate limited genuine concern for employee welfare, and tend to accept their highly paid CEO's version of events without consulting bullied employees. In such organisations, there are many different sections and locations, some strangled by tradition, bureaucracy or hierarchy. Company directors and senior executives have blind spots to the inappropriate practices perpetuated by middle management and those lower down. Their lack of a 'hands-on' approach stops them pursing the appropriate implementation of bullying-prevention policies. Thus while senior executives in their granite and marble designer offices value feedback from climate surveys and 360-degree feedback, their middle-level manager remains oblivious. He bullies those below who depend upon his support for their livelihood and career, while he plays up to those above him, telling them what they want to hear. Thus organisations avoid responsibility and accountability, and lack consistency in dealing with bullying.

Condition 3: The target is different

> *'I was a highly trained secondary teacher, whereas most of their teachers are primary teachers, who didn't like it or couldn't do it. Maybe that is where some of the bullying problems lie. They are sent to the "easy" areas of adult teaching, where unqualified or underperforming teachers can be protected by clique membership.'*

People like people who are most like them. Employers generally reflect their local community attitudes, traditions, culture and values. Therefore, they may be threatened by those who are different or vulnerable — such as the only female, older person, social isolate, migrant, religious minority or homosexual — so they attack or exclude them. Some are bullied following jealousy about their wealth, social status or international travel, or a physical injury that affects their work.

Blame the target

> *People explain their actions by blaming environmental factors, not their own behaviours. But when assessing other people's behaviours, they blame their personality, rather than environmental factors.[5]*

Surviving in the work jungle is difficult. It's easier to blame a few employees than confront bigger organisational problems such as systemic failures. Having a common scapegoat builds teamwork; the manager who is feeling threatened by serious work stresses or wanting to avoid conflict simplifies their job by blaming someone who stands out as different and who has become vulnerable, instead of confronting a threatening, manipulative bully. The quiet achiever or atypical employee is an easier focus for stressed, frustrated, less competent managers than challenging the underlying causes. They find it safer to target petty incidents or personal problems than to investigate abuse, fraud, mismanagement or other inappropriate activities.

Gender issues

'You have to fit into your gender role or you'll be bullied.'

Although men and women can be targets or bullies, there are differences in the way these roles are carried out. Throughout history, and still today despite the rise of feminism, the majority of women have less personal and economic power. They are more vulnerable physically, less powerful orally and occupy less body space than males. In fact, the most subtle, passive-aggressive type of bullying today might be the formal and informal exclusion of many women from all forms of power — education, economic security, career and status. Women have traditionally been seen as nurturers and gatherers who network in small groups to connect, relate and bond together. They tend to say 'We did this together'. While focusing upon collaboration and building relationships, they view confrontation as sabotage and therefore make greater concessions to preserve relationships. The traditional female role is to be friendly and caring, so they're more likely to support others and be attacked for doing so. Women are still expected by many to be subservient and obey their father-figure manager.

The female manager who uses a collaborative management style and says 'We did this together' may not be regarded as successful as the male who advertises any achievement he's remotely affiliated with by claiming 'I did this'. Cultural conditioning still makes it difficult for women to be assertive and confrontational, some survive by being passive-aggressive and using tactics such as malicious rumours and exclusion, while some misconstrue aggression for assertiveness. When women executives overcome countless hurdles to join the boys' club or transcend the glass ceiling, they are expected to conform and become more aggressive. Often society's double standard labels mean male bullies as 'go-getters' and women bosses as 'bitches'. When women feel powerless, they internalise, becoming depressed and paralysed. Evidence shows that they suffer trauma more deeply than men.

In contrast, men have traditionally been seen as hunters who appear to regard relationships as competitive and based upon power and dominance. They deny their feelings for others, especially empathy. Since childhood many have not been educated to understand emotions, and are encouraged to hide behind a mask of bravado.[6] They find it hard to identify and communicate their feelings, which handicaps their ability to develop close relationships. Anger is often the only emotion allowed and condoned, but they don't know how to release it assertively. At work, if they are aggressive, they are respected as competitive. They don't confront their emotional difficulties, but discuss their achievements, numbers or sport. When faced with conflict they bottle up their feelings, lose their temper, or escape to their cave. Men use office politics and large networks to build powerful coalitions or boys' clubs. In this bullying game the *hunters* exclude the *gatherers*.

Cultural differences

> The lights went out in the office of a computer company in India. The bully tried to rape the receptionist, believing it acceptable in India. His American multinational employer thought otherwise and dismissed him.

The tribe respects those who blend together. However, workplace bullying varies around the world. It is subtler in Scandinavia and more overt in countries such as the United Kingdom, South Africa, United States, Australia and New Zealand. Although bullying can certainly be a part of racial discrimination, even in countries with a history of racist difficulties, most bullying involves a target and perpetrator of the same colour.[7] Some cultures do confront conflict differently. Asians may appear less assertive because they are taught to be more respectful, value interpersonal harmony and avoid confrontation. North Americans focus on physical violence at work as a main concern rather than workplace bullying. Even though more people are bullied at work, greater legislation is targeted at workplace homicide.[8]

Condition 4: Poor ethical standards

When employees are treated without respect, the work atmosphere can become stressful, confrontational, competitive and dangerous. It appears that when business practices are negligent, corrupt or fraudulent, the incidence of bullying increases as employees try to rectify a problem.

Likewise, employers who neglect obvious physical-safety issues are less likely to be concerned about bullying and its toxic impact. Although occupational health and safety legislation or guidelines for dealing with workplace bullying are becoming more prevalent, there is a huge gap between legal requirements and actual enforcement. In most countries it is very difficult to make an employer accountable for employees who have been bullied, or to prosecute these cases.

The work culture

> In a major British study (1997), Dr Charlotte Rayner found identical results for bullied and nonbullied employees; 95% of workers are too scared to report, 84% say the 'bully has done this before' and 73% said that 'management knew about it'.[9]

The authoritarian approach that was once seen as useful in rebuilding the world's economy after World War II has now shifted to a more democratic style of management. Unfortunately, the traditional authoritarian approach lingers in some organisations, such as public service, medicine, nursing, education, and the apprenticeship system. While most managers wouldn't be caught dead with a 3-year-old mobile phone, some employ out-of-date leadership styles that foster unproductive bully tactics.

Building a resilient organisational culture is based upon openness, diversity and a willingness to challenge the status quo.[10] Unfortunately, these qualities are sabotaged when survival becomes the norm; so in a stressful, dysfunctional work culture, people aren't respected. In fact, like a battered wife, some employees are groomed to accept abuse and their colleagues are constrained by a conspiracy of silence. A bully can conceal his incompetencies and unethical practices while he pursues promotion, purchases power and plays politics using the bullying as a diversionary tactic.

Nevertheless, bullying only survives within a culture that allows it, regardless of the personalities of either target or bully. Bullies rely on the implicit support of management, while the target has to shape up or ship out. When there is a history of bullying in the company it acts like a cultural template for the bullying to continue. The impact flows down the line like hot lava, hurting all in its wake.

Bystander betrayal

> *'Their barrister claimed that Mary did not like me; I showed him the recent Christmas card she sent me.'*

Many people witness bullying but are scared to stand up and support the target, because they believe that they will be targeted next. Some would like to support the victim but don't know what to say to the bully, HR or management. These silent witnesses perpetuate bullying by their inaction, whereas others are supportive right up to the moment they have to give a witness statement for an investigator and are then bullied by management to turn against their friend.

Fraud, malpractice and other unethical and illegal activities

> *John bullied 17 people out of the company. He hides this from the board because they'll discover he's fiddling government funding.*

Senior leaders create the culture of the organisation. Although a small percentage of bullies have an antisocial personality disorder, most depend upon incompetent or corrupt managers and their organisations to condone or sponsor their counterproductive work behaviours. In organisations with limited accountability, fraud, mismanagement and bullying can escalate.

Managers may use some form of social intimidation to divert attention away from their illegal activities, prevent staff questioning unethical practices, and reduce reporting. Conscientious employees, with high expectations of themselves and others, who witness malpractices pose a threat to bullies, whom they could report to appropriate authorities. Therefore, any form of malpractice constitutes an excellent reason to eliminate a potential threat by bullying them out, such as occurred at the giant bankrupted US telecommunications firm Enron before its collapse.

Whistleblowers

The majority of whistleblowers aren't troublemakers. They generally prefer to conform rather than challenge authority but interpret unethical behaviours within their organisation as a betrayal of a fair value system. They show an amazing degree of courage to expose malpractice, corruption and other unethical practices, but they can receive some very negative responses to their actions.

I know of a well-known surgeon who challenged the 'medical boys' club' when he reported surgical errors and mistakes in patient care, including his own. Some of the bullying behaviours he experienced were:

- 'I don't believe in this new procedure because *you* thought about it first.'
- failure to get research grants when others did
- refusal to allow him to participate in transplants
- waiting lists being changed without his permission
- lack of patient referrals from other departments
- malicious rumours being spread about his personality, mental state and professional abilities.

The way in which a whistleblower is treated reflects the level of corruption within the organisation. Like the canary down the coalmine, their health is as an early sign of difficulty within the organisation.[11] Although whistle-blowers identify the evils within their company, paradoxically, most are oblivious to the dangers facing them. Two-thirds of employees who spoke out against mistreatment faced some form of retaliation from their harassers.[12] Many fear for their safety and, in some countries, their lives are actually at risk. Despite legislation, they experience informal and formal retaliation, including bullying; thus whistleblowing damages their health, wellbeing and career.

CHAPTER FIVE

The toxic effects
of workplace bullying

❝*I managed a large tertiary teaching department in a college known for bullying competent women. When I supported a female colleague by reporting her bully to the Board, I was warned I'd be next. I'm not a rebel and didn't go looking for trouble. Soon after, management gave me an unrealistic workload and applied fraudulent accounting procedures to devalue me personally and professionally.*

The bullying burnt me out slowly and I fell into a 'black hole'. I became depressed, anxious and traumatised. Although I'd often spoken publicly, my voice went and I stuttered. I'd lose my front door key and panic without my mobile phone. I couldn't sleep. Sometimes I asked my sister to hold me. I felt ugly and unattractive, as my hair and eyebrows fell out. I was terrified I'd lost my mind and would be locked up. My psychiatrist, concerned about early dementia, sent me for a brain scan. I had suicidal thoughts.

I moved house but was scared to drive far. My doctor referred me to a local psychologist interested in workplace bullying. Slowly we identified and released my pain, I stopped blaming myself and rebuilt my health and self-esteem. I organised all the evidence to take my former employer and 16 staff to the Equal Opportunity Commission.

It's taken four years to find new directions. My hair has regrown, my voice returned and my concentration skills are good. I still stutter when anxious. I'll never return to my career or recoup what I've lost financially. ❞

Being bullied is like being stuck between a rock and a hard place. During sustained abuse you switch off and disconnect from what's really happening. You find it difficult to identify its evil nature as it grows, revealing nasty tentacles of abuse, public humiliation, injury and damage. When you are constantly bullied, blamed and branded, you begin to either fall apart or implode. When you internalise your emotional pain, you can become a shell of a person. Something inside of you changes and your confidence curdles. Then it's too late. You have lost the energy to prevent it, the opportunity to confront it effectively or leave with a good reference.

Like other sustained complex traumas, bullying initiates a domino effect. Your primary damage is further exacerbated by secondary factors. This dominates nearly everything else in your life and leads to many layers and levels of damage. Everything can fall apart for years. You can experience incredible social, psychological and physical injuries.

Although you may have spent years developing a personal and professional identity that you were proud of and was valued by many others, slowly it is twisted into a foreign shape, totally different to your former self. Bullying attacks your identity, so you begin to believe that everyone is judging you differently. Thus you are altered emotionally and physically, publicly and privately, personally and professionally, socially and individually.

Ultimately a severe bullying experience alters the way you view the world. If your survival instinct is unable to take control, you are powerless, unable to act, and your level of fear and anger intensifies. You feel even more betrayed, sabotaged and abandoned. The more protracted the bullying process, the greater the likelihood of injury. Each stressful event harms you further and delays your recovery. It is a form of psychic death. I often wonder what's not affected, rather than what is.

The bullying experience

> 'If it were a punch on the nose, you'd have a chance. But when it's a dripping tap, almost always under the radar, it not only really harms you, but in my case, it has left me very shaken. I have eight years' university education and I didn't see this coming or happening; all I knew was that hurtful and unpleasant or bizarre or unfair things happened often and out of the blue; always with no explanation or rationale ... Despite repeated attempts, I could not find out why this was happening — that was one of the cruellest aspects of all.'

The real difficulty for everyone involved in a case of bullying is to identify and stop the bully game before it gets out of control. You may not realise you are being targeted until you are entangled in the conflict. You may be unaware of the toxic nature of bullying and seriously injured long before you identify and acknowledge it.

What targets say:

'I had two choices — wear it or shut up.'

'New staff are built up, burned out and bullied out.'

'The bully bullies below and curries favour to those above.'

'I went from the frying pan into the fire and was bullied again.'

'I've seen him ruin peoples' lives.'

'Nothing I did stopped the bullying. I felt stripped naked.'

'Did she act out of malice or stupidity?'

'I thought it would end soon and they'd be friendly again.'

'How can I prove it when it is so subtle and devious?'

'He accused me of undermining!'

'My legs couldn't take me to work anymore, I was too sick to fill out the insurance form.'

'I've been to hell and back and have no skills to deal with it.'

'Why does the target have to see a psychiatrist, not the bully?'

While bullying may propel you into a report-and-confront mode, if the bullying masquerades as 'general business practice' or 'improving productivity', your managers may condone this behaviour. They can sabotage your search for justice, thereby exacerbating your experience of bullying. You are compelled to use the informal grapevine network or legal measures instead of legitimate collaborative or dispute resolution procedures. Unfortunately, many bullying targets find it difficult to present a logical, sequential, coherent description of the bullying. While you obsess about details, you leave out chunks of your story; therefore those with power to intervene are less likely to believe your story and assist you. You may then experience higher levels of stress, depression and trauma. Instead of tackling ordinary work requirements or new challenges, you concentrate upon survival and obtaining support for your case. Sadly, you have less time to network or work with colleagues.

If your attempts are fruitless, you will lose concentration and disassociate emotionally. Your self-confidence deteriorates and you may become less capable of applying for another job. Although some bullying targets find a safe retreat by moving sideways, others are forced to leave. Some are successful; others are too injured to work for years. Unfortunately, many victims may only identify the chain of events that created and sustained the bullying some years after they find validation and have moved on.

Bullying is a social and physical injury

It is well known that when people face stress, loss or trauma, they cope better with a social support network. Social interaction and connection are actually a basic survival need, just as necessary as food or water. Human beings evolved as a species by belonging to their tribe; being rejected represents starvation and death. Losing your social identity, social and professional status and social networks threatens your basic survival.

Thus, real or threatened social rejection is extremely painful. In fact, research shows that physical and social pain is similar in 'experience, function, and underlying neural structure'.[1] Not only are you abused, you experience shame and social stigma that ostracises and isolates you from external social support as well as from your internal, established identity, which slowly disintegrates. Thus you are attacked internally and externally. Bullying at work constitutes a basic threat to your life, in many different ways. It can create physical, psychological and social pain and many different types of injury.

The impact of workplace bullying on the target

> Mary was a competent senior teacher who was bullied by the department head. She's too scared to return to teaching. She couldn't hold a conversation, became sensitive to noise, suffered from skin problems and diarrhoea. She ground her teeth at night and experienced headaches. She slept for 2 to 3 hours at a time and couldn't drive for about 8 months. She can't paint anymore although she's talented. She's depressed and anxious. She still feels enraged and describes it as the 'creeping danger' because she didn't realise that her body was slowly breaking down. She shopped for unnecessary items and gambled to cope.

Bullying at work is a complicated injury. Although single events can be very traumatic, they are different to sustained chronic abuse such as domestic violence and child sexual abuse. In addition, whereas the latter suffer private shame, workplace bullying attacks your social identity, causing social rejection and creating public humiliation.

When a person is physically injured they need urgent transport to hospital. This increases their chance of survival, reduces further injury and recuperation time. Similarly, the workplace bullying target requires immediate acknowledgment, validation and safety. Tragically, this doesn't often happen and the victim continues to suffer the injurious consequences, with a prolonged recovery.

Physical impact

Stress and trauma can directly or indirectly impact on your health (e.g., alter thyroid function; trigger diabetes, heart disease, cancer and stroke). Some victims are affected by side effects from their medication, smoking and alcohol abuse, or physical and car/bicycle accidents. The physical consequences of bullying can include:

- minor infections, reduced immune functioning, autoimmune illness
- sleep difficulties, nightmares, night sweats, teeth grinding, clenched jaws
- stomach problems (e.g., heartburn, acid stomach, vomiting, flatulence, nausea, constipation, diarrhoea, irritable bowel syndrome)
- eating problems (e.g., weight gain, diabetes)
- speech difficulties (e.g., stuttering, forgetting, mixing words, voice alteration)
- high blood pressure, shortness of breath, fatigue, migraines, dizziness, palpitations
- muscular skeletal problems (e.g., headaches, back pain, chest pain) tremors, trembling)

- allergies, skin problems, cold sores, hair loss, chronic fatigue, impotence
- self-abuse (mutilation), suicide attempts, suicide.

Psychological impact

The psychological consequences of bullying are also wide ranging and include:

- extreme anxiety, frenetic behaviour, nervous twitches
- obsessive thoughts (e.g., constantly reviewing bullying incidents)
- anger, humiliation, shame
- paranoia, hypervigilance, hypersensitivity, avoidance of danger (e.g., fear of meeting the bully)
- depression, tearfulness, withdrawal, suicidal feelings, mood swings
- shock, numbness, helplessness, powerlessness, burnout, paralysis
- sadness and grief for numerous losses.

Once targeted, you may feel overwhelmed by the magnitude and complexity of these strange, unwelcome bullying experiences. Your confusion and intense pain creates a deep hole of torment. Your fight or flight survival instinct, which generally protects and empowers you, slowly implodes under the intense pressure. Your biochemical stress-regulating hormonal system becomes overloaded. You don't have enough cortisol to regulate your high level of arousal and deal with the prolonged stress.[2] Your symptoms grow like a time bomb ready to explode, leading to burnout and breakdown.

If your perception of reality and the events you experience is challenged, denied or nullified, you question your feelings, thought processes and experiences; for example: *Why can't they believe me? I was an excellent worker for years, why do they suddenly pick on my minor mistakes? I loved this job, how can they take it from me?*

When your reality is denied, you feel sabotaged. You are brainwashed by the bully, his gang, your former workmates and your employer into losing your professional confidence and work identity. Your personality and self-hood are split and fragmented, you collapse, curdle or crumble. Your whole being can experience an internal destruction that resembles a total disintegration of your former self.

You are more likely to be injured if you have experienced a major threat to your life, extreme horror, powerlessness, guilt, professional shame (betrayal, stigma), endured other stresses, have limited personal, professional and social support, or were overcommitted to the job.

The impact of the bullying is exacerbated by the variety, length and intensity of the experiences. Your vulnerability to trauma injury is exacerbated by witnessing others being bullied (secondary trauma), or having experienced earlier abuse such as domestic violence or school bullying. Any lack of validation by your employer, insurers, lawyers, and others will be experienced as a continuation of the bullying and aggravate your level of injury.

Mental health professionals use many different labels, including severe depression, anxiety disorder, social phobia, adjustment disorder and post-traumatic stress disorder. This is why I have chosen the term 'workplace bullying trauma'.

Later on, when the danger subsides, your brain may have difficulty distinguishing between trauma and stress. You can react as though you are confronting a real trauma when it is just an everyday problem. This could happen in your family, socially or at your next job. An innocuous event can bring back awful memories, such that life becomes a game of 'snakes and ladders', where small triggers set off flashbacks that sabotage your recovery.

Stress hormones affect your ability to think, comprehend, concentrate, analyse, create, remember, learn and solve problems at work or in your private life. Under stress your judgment may be less accurate, tasks take longer and you make minor errors. Understanding written material — whether it is a magazine, book or legal document — is extremely difficult if you are traumatised, stressed or depressed.

When you relate your bullying story, there will inevitably be holes in it due to stress. Your memory of details may be hazy and haphazard. Thus you need to file all your information together and maintain your record. Then make a summary; otherwise your poor memory will frustrate anyone trying to help you.

Personality change

> Prior to the bullying Maria had a happy, outgoing, confident personality: 'I felt as though my personality had been killed off. I was afraid to act like myself. I changed into an angry, scared, introverted and depressed person. Suddenly I felt a failure and experienced overwhelming feelings of desperation. I cried for hours when no one was around.'

Many targets describe their personality as being altered by the bullying; for example, *I'm different now. I finder it harder to trust people. I enjoy things less. I can't have fun. I can't control my feelings as I did before.* Suddenly, you have difficulty dealing with your emotions, which emulate a rollercoaster. You become more sensitive and obsess about your bully experiences and the repercussions, often for years. Fear of further danger leads you to paranoid thinking, a fear of trusting others and, consequently, social isolation. If you had been friendly and outgoing, you may become introverted. Suddenly, you doubt your own skills and abilities, even if you have worked successfully for decades. In contrast to your previous independence and initiative, you develop an overwhelming sense of self-doubt. Like many other traumas, bullying can instigate a life-altering, personality-changing experience. You can become a different person.

Self-esteem loss

> Jack doesn't know who he is anymore. He's lost his purpose in life, his self-esteem and social life. He doesn't contact people because he doesn't know what to talk about. He knew management was bad, but thought he'd be safe if he did his work.
> He blames himself for not doing more. He said he would rather fight in a war where he could identify the enemy.

Regardless of whether you are a surgeon or a chef's apprentice, most people construct an identity based on their work. Any threat to your employment threatens your survival needs and your self-esteem. Systematic, prolonged bullying undermines your self-confidence. Having reached a stage where you might have been enjoying a sense of personal and professional achievement, you then experience deep feelings of guilt, humiliation, shame and embarrassment.

- Although it's unfair and unreasonable, you say, *I'm to blame, I must have done something wrong;* or you're ashamed — *I should have stopped the bullying game.* You blame yourself for not knowing why and how it happened, because you need time, distance and objectivity to do that.

- Experiencing malicious rumours (e.g., 'Gina can't cope with too much work', 'Fred had a breakdown') adds the shame of social stigma and further undermines your reputation and self-image.

- Your self-esteem deteriorates, you feel devalued and a failure and lose confidence in your ability to function normally (e.g., *I don't feel worthy enough to obtain a good job after being humiliated*).

- Sadly, you may find it very difficult to believe that others still regard you as a good person, who is competent, capable and employable.

Altered beliefs

> 'I felt like a torture victim undergoing mind control techniques. They said, "See things our way, do things our way. If you don't, we'll make you. If you continue to resist we will humiliate and disempower you, until you submit or exit". If you resist, it becomes a challenge. This becomes a battle of wills about your fundamental character. This became a deep trauma for me because my basic belief in myself and my society was sabotaged. To concede and submit meant a fundamental change in my core beliefs, everything I'd built my life around. It meant "giving up myself" and becoming somebody strange and foreign.'

A dramatic event can shatter your basic assumptions about the world, yourself and others. The universal forces of evil and injustice compel you to confront your personal vulnerability and powerlessness. Psychologist Janoff-Bulman sees the process of trauma effects along a timeline of deteriorating personal assumptions.[3]

- You start out believing that the world is a good and safe place (e.g., *I'll get justice.*).
- Then you are forced to abandon these naive beliefs (e.g., *My employer and workmates aren't doing the right thing by me.*).
- Your lifelong beliefs and expectations are shattered (e.g., *I can't control my life. I'm powerless. Things aren't OK.*).
- You discard your internal sense of competence (e.g., *I can't handle any challenge. I'm a failure.*).
- You believe that your reputation is injured (e.g., *People don't respect me anymore.*).
- You lose your belief in human rights (e.g., *There's no justice.*).

Furthermore, the lack of acknowledgment by your adversarial employer, lack of support from sloppy managers, fearful colleagues and inept professionals damages you further. Finally, when your employer fears legal liability, they may pressure you to settle out of court with a comprehensive gagging clause. This stops you sharing your story and receiving validation from others.

Loss of social relationships

> Scott can't trust his work colleagues anymore. He's stopped being friendly at work or socialising outside office hours. Everyone's scared to support one another, as their own job may suffer repercussions or they fear being bullied next.

Work is a great place to socialise and develop friendships. These relationships create a supportive network, facilitate a positive work environment and enhance productivity. Once established, some friendships move into your personal life and you remain good friends long after leaving a job.

When you are bullied you tend to socialise less at work as well as privately. You become socially vigilant to avoid painful social encounters. You may want to avoid meeting your bully, and most colleagues move away or reject you with statements such as 'I can't believe that', or 'He treats everyone the same, don't worry'. Perhaps a few supported you originally but backed off later, scared of losing their job or threatened themselves by the bully. Regardless of their reasons, you feel abandoned and betrayed.

It is also hard to maintain your private social life — to go out and have fun. It is very difficult to switch off from work worries and to participate in the chitchat and any sharing of empathy that is mandatory for maintaining friendships. You may avoid close friends to stop burdening them with your need to obsess about the bullying. You may feel embarrassed to show them how you have been affected, or feel it is painful being with friends who don't understand. Others may avoid you because they cannot cope with your high levels of stress, anger and depression. Unfortunately, if you lose contact with friends at work, personal friends and extended family, you become more isolated and depressed.

Career damage

> 'I loved teaching and I miss it every day, but it ruined my life, as it did others' — outstanding, sincere, hardworking people really decimated by the horrific dynamics in an undervalued sector. A former student of mine asked recently, 'Are they still cutting teachers' legs off there?'

At first you work harder to prove your motivation and comply with the job requirements. However, the bully or manager may sabotage your work, or your emotional stress may begin to affect your job performance. Mistakes can damage your career and reduced motivation sabotages your chances of promotion. Your colleagues help until fear or frustration forces them to abandon you. You can become so focused upon proving your innocence that you forget to protect yourself and then isolation affects your career.

Unfortunately, when your confidence is eroded, it is hard to apply for another job and handle the interview process. It is difficult to explain why you left your previous position because being the target of workplace bullying is not generally acceptable and job applicants are normally penalised for being negative about their previous employer. Besides, your employer can sabotage you further by refusing to give a reasonable reference or using grapevine gossip to undermine your future career prospects. Many targets find it too traumatic to return to the same type of work and older employees may find it difficult to obtain full-time permanent, employment. You may work part-time, semi-retire, move to another industry or work for yourself. Some targets will never work again.

Financial costs

> *Barry decided to expand his successful company by bringing in a partner, who then bullied him out, despite the fact that he held 50% of shares. He was forced to settle for thousands less than his entitlement. He felt rejected by his wife, which then triggered his affair with Mary, his 'beacon of positiveness'. His divorce set him back financially and the planned early retirement has been postponed indefinitely.*

Bullying can affect you financially, in many different ways. You can lose holiday pay and sick leave; receive reduced overtime payments, lower staff benefits, and less income from loss of promotions; and suffer the loss of a second job. Workers compensation or unemployment benefits are far less than your salary and your superannuation will reduce with forced earlier retirement. You may have less funds to meet medical expenses and maintain financial commitments (e.g., mortgage) that can snowball, leaving you with increased debt. You may have to forgo small luxuries and juggle your finances, and if you have concentration difficulties, it may be difficult for you to manage your affairs. Any litigation you undertake can be extremely expensive. According to psychologists Ruth and Gary Namie,[4] half of all bullying targets lose some or all of their income, a third move on with no financial change, and one-sixth obtain a better salary elsewhere.

Family/marital issues

> *After five years of bullying Jillian is still depressed. She hasn't felt like having sex with her husband since the bullying began. She*

> *misses their former emotional intimacy, her husband has become impotent and both miss the sex. Her children are sick and tired of hearing her talk about her workplace. They're frustrated that she's less involved in their life.*

Bullying can damage your relationship with your partner or family who normally provides you with vital emotional, social, physical and financial support. They care for you and help you cope with your anger, depression and trauma. Yet, they are under pressure to repair your recently damaged, fragile self-esteem. They bear the brunt of your frustration and powerlessness if you project your anger and fear onto them, then spend longer at work to avoid being home with you, or displace their frustration onto other activities. Some people may even lose wages themselves while caring for their victimised partner. If your income is not essential to the family finances, then your partner may have difficulty understanding why the bullying was such a huge issue for you. Your children may blame themselves and suffer learning difficulties and emotional problems if they don't receive the understanding, nurturing and support they require.

Extended family members may find it hard to believe your story — *Where there's smoke there's fire* — creating a rift. Sometimes you will avoid family so they don't see how the bullying has affected you. If your family doesn't understand what workplace bullying involves or has difficulty coping with problems, this will increase your trauma and delay your recovery. Beware: severe strain may lead to breakdown, separation and divorce.

Secondary effects of workplace bullying

When you report the bullying to a dysfunctional organisation — one that is not prepared to handle such events — it defends itself by minimising incidents or retaliating. Instead of being regarded as having a workplace injury, you are blamed, shamed and stigmatised. The bully is generally protected (until you are out of the way) while you are labelled the problem, or even sometimes accused of being the bully yourself! You may be described as having a personality problem, a communication difficulty or a mental illness. They may blame you for being ineffective, or create a minor infringement to sack you. When management and colleagues betray you and your organisation rejects a fair resolution, you experience a greater sense of failure. This organisational level of mistrust and betrayal may be only the first instance of a series of wider debilitating effects of your workplace bullying experience.

Some facts about workplace trauma victims

- *75% of victims experience trauma, with higher scores than traditional trauma victims.[5]*
- *65% of victims had symptoms five years later.[6]*
- *Targets can be affected in other significant areas of their life (e.g., family, friends, leisure, sex, [12% no impact, 50% moderate damage, 38% severe impairment])[7]*
- *Targets have lower levels of cortisol in their saliva than non-bullied employees at work, and are less able to cope with stress.[8]*
- *Posttraumatic stress symptoms are significantly higher among current victims of bullying than previous victims or witnesses, therefore victims do improve.[9]*

Professional lack of understanding

> *'My psychiatrist said I was suffering from an anxiety disorder, he gave me a prescription for antidepressants, told me to get over it and find another job.'*

Dealing with workplace bullying is a recent area of study and practice. Many mental health practitioners confuse it with chronic stress, a totally different biochemical disorder.[10] There is no current diagnosis for workplace bullying trauma, and many victims receive inappropriate, inadequate diagnoses that may sabotage their treatment. There is limited research about effective models of treatment. Many doctors, psychologists and psychiatrists have limited opportunities to understand the extensive damage caused by workplace bullying; few obtain appropriate training to research, understand and develop effective skills. The current obsession with some forms of brief therapy does not take into account the continuing pattern of abuse, such as regular flashbacks and subsequent legal action by the employer's insurers over many years. Thus the professional ignorance of therapists who lack understanding and empathy, provide brief sessions, solely prescribe drugs or blame you, will victimise you further and sabotage your recovery. You are forced to remain longer in the healthcare system, because the psychomedical system fails to diagnose and treat you effectively.

The medico–legal treadmill

> *Jill regarded every visit to a medico–legal professional as traumatic. The night before, she found it even more difficult to sleep, cried a lot and felt nauseous. She was very scared, realising that her entire future depended upon this psychiatrist's assessment. She often left feeling blamed and unacknowledged.*

When you need an income, such as workers compensation, medical treatment or any other form of justice and compensation available within your legal system, you require a medico–legal assessment. Your employer, their insurance company and lawyer or your lawyer will send you to a psychiatrist/psychologist for a medical opinion. This may try to prove whether the bullying occurred (which is difficult without witnesses) or assess your injuries (which is hard without evidence-based diagnostic criteria). Then you will encounter the frustrating merry-go-round of regularly visiting doctors, psychiatrists, psychologists and lawyers. Their professional neutrality may surface as indifference. The interview process may be too brief to give the whole story. Some may seem to intimidate you with tactics resembling your bullying. When you are forced to see medico–legal practitioners who are unskilled, biased or manipulated by insurance companies and forget their ethical responsibilities to you and their profession, you will be further injured.

Time is a killer

> *Unlike litigants in some countries, Ruth receives Workcover insurance from her employer until she leaves the system or settles. She has to see a different psychiatrist every six months, and she often asks her union to ask her employer to rectify mistakes in her pay. Ruth has had to confront many legal steps along the gauntlet and has been waiting for over seven years to go to court.*

Unlike restorative systems and other collaborative practices, investigation, mediation and conciliation processes have the potential to drag out a resolution for months. You are regularly exposed to triggers that force you to relive painful events. If you are forced to leave work, employers can make mistakes or even sabotage your payout. You are forced to have further contact with them until your obtain all your financial entitlements. You wait years for a medical insurance panel to make decisions and then take your case to court. The whole process causes further damage.

Insurance companies only settle when your condition has stabilised. This can take years and you may well find yourself stuck waiting for a

Checklist — Are your symptoms consistent with workplace bullying trauma?

How often and how long did you experience bullying behaviours?

Do you experience physical difficulties, especially sleep or eating disorders?

Are you showing emotional signs? For example, irritability, tearfulness, anxiety, panic attacks, depression, numbness?

Do you constantly obsess about what happened?

Are you constantly angry at the lack of validation and justice?

Has your concentration, motivation and quality of work been affected?

Has your confidence and spiritual life been affected by bullying?

Are you scared of being near anything that reminds you of the bullying?

Is the bullying affecting your job or career?

Do you experience a financial impact? For example, worse shifts, fewer customers?

Are there negative changes in your social and recreational life?

Are your family relationships affected?

Are the dispute investigation, legal and medico–legal processes having a detrimental impact on you?

resolution before you can get on with your life. You cannot heal while you wait because you need the public validation from the legal action to heal emotionally. Because validation will not occur until your medical condition has stabilised, you are stuck between a rock and a hard place!

Bullying affects witnesses

> *Kate likes Jenny, her manager, but dislikes Jenny's bullying of the younger women. Although she tries to confront Jenny, Kate feels caught in the middle. Her time is spent resolving conflicts, not working.*

Although bullies may believe that bullying is a popular spectator sport, much like reality television, observing bullying is actually a distracting, draining and

Don't be a bully

Although bullying behaviours might achieve your short-term goals, going ballistic will boomerang back on you. Bullying disguises interpersonal incompetence. Many bullies are notoriously unreliable because they cannot regulate their emotions, perform their job requirements and handle feedback. They sabotage safe, creative, productive working environments. You risk retaliation or having staff undermine your performance. You can be blamed for management difficulties, lose credibility and be sued.

Unfortunately, you may be rewarded and promoted until you are too hot to handle. One day you could find yourself at the end of a shooting gallery. Your employer may need another scapegoat, or wish to minimise possible costs associated with bullying, including litigation and/or bad publicity. Despite having encouraged and promoted you, suddenly they change direction. Then you are confronted with some evidence, moved aside or dismissed without appropriate support or retraining, often at the height of your career. Alternatively, you get away with bullying for years, but once you reach a senior executive level, your targets find the collective confidence to attack, using your higher status as leverage. Exposure is embarrassing, debilitating and devastating. You can be victimised, devalued, denied natural justice and humiliated. Ultimately your career, financial status and self-esteem can adversely be affected!

distressing process. Everyone in a bullying workplace becomes self-protective and uses their energies to survive, instead of being productive and creative. Many bystanders show increased physiological arousal long after the bullying ceases, as bullying affects their emotional and physical health.

Nobody enjoys being bullied, and when you witness bullying you become aware of your own powerlessness to stop the game and help the target. You may try to take action but felt frustrated and undermined when your ignorant employer does not intervene effectively. As you witness colleagues slowly change from healthy people into injured victims, you may begin to fear it is your turn next on the firing line. It can become difficult to help your bullied colleague, and you may even be pressured to betray them to keep your job.

Witnesses are constantly forced to gauge what is happening around them and alter their behaviours to protect themselves. If the bullying camouflages fraud and malpractice, there will be further deterioration in office productivity and these changes can damage your professional profile and future career prospects.

Bully boomerangs

The Australian boomerang is a thin hardwood missile that is designed to kill animals and return in a circle to its thrower. If thrown poorly, it can recoil on the thrower, wounding him. I use the term 'bully boomerangs' to highlight the dangers of reacting to bullying with such aggression or mismanagement that instead of leading to a resolution of the problem further damage is done.

> The professor was a good surgeon. When senior surgeons made complaints about his aggressive management style and fee structure, senior executives dismissed them and bullied whistleblowers. A few years later, when the 'shit hit the fan', he was publicly outed by the media. Had the hospital listened to the original complaints and taken appropriate action, everyone would have experienced less humiliation and distress.

> Julie is a competent professional woman. She was horrified, ashamed and humiliated when she faced the internal investigation and confronted about her bullying behaviours. She was unaware that she'd been doing anything wrong and was deeply upset by the accusations. She had difficulty coping, had sleepless nights and developed a nervous rash. It affected her marriage. A closer look showed that she was manipulated by a rigid authoritarian work system and bullied by her own CEO.

Remember that most people can be a target or bully. A bully's behaviour may seem inconsequential, entertaining or rewarding to them. They may not even be aware that these behaviours are offensive, or they may believe that bullying is a better way to get ahead. They can be insensitive to the fact that these behaviours have caused their target to feel humiliated, scapegoated or forced to resign, and ignorant of the injuries instigated.

The impact of workplace bullying on organisations

> In 2000, Cerner Corporation, a leading US supplier of healthcare technology, was listed in Fortune magazine's 100 best

> companies to work for in America. In April 2001, the CEO sent
> an angry email to 400 managers. 'We are getting less than 40
> hours of work from a large number of our EMPLOYEES ... As
> managers, you either do not know what your EMPLOYEES are
> doing or you do not CARE ... you have a problem and you will
> fix it or I will replace you. NEVER in my career have I allowed a
> team which worked for me to think they had a 40-hour job'. His
> tirade continued, adding that hell would freeze over before he
> increased employee benefits. The missive concluded, 'You have
> two weeks. Tick, tock'. Someone posted it on a Yahoo financial
> message board. Within hours the company's shares plummeted
> 22% amid fears by investors that employee morale would
> plummet!

When one part of a hanging mobile moves in the wind, the other parts also move. If an organisation wins a fantastic contract or is nominated dealer of the year, everyone shares the success. If a valued employee has a life-threatening illness, the feeling of loss pervades their workplace. Similarly, bullying creates emotions of fear, anger and powerlessness that permeate the organisation like the smell of burning sulfur.

When a board of management tolerate bullying they release a downward, destructive spiral, which influences their whole company. Bullying has a disruptive impact on corporate values and organisational culture, essential for sustaining and promoting business. It is a reflection of psychologically unhealthy people and organisations[11] and a sign of dysfunctional power, poor leadership and a toxic culture. Although dealing with stress and conflict at work is an occupational hazard, in dysfunctional organisations, bullying results in psychological and physical abuse that damages the entire organisation.

Incompetence in bullies and targets

> 'My corporate bully targeted anybody who threatened her by
> being more competent than her. I realised afterwards that the
> three people in our organisation who were bullied were the most
> competent. My fate was sealed when I was introduced by the
> CEO who said, 'If you need to know anything ask Tania because
> she knows everything'. She immediately made organisational
> changes, such as getting a personal assistant to block direct
> contact with her. The previous CEO had worked for 7 years
> without one and was no busier. But she built a wall around
> herself and had someone else to blame for mistakes.'

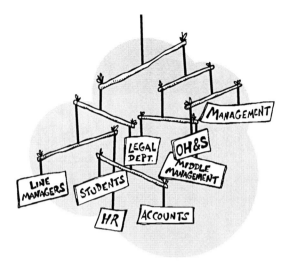

Like everyone else, some targets may have performance and discipline issues that require skilled intervention. However, it is not necessary to bully an incompetent person. They should be identified early and told to leave, improve or move to an area where their inadequacies are tolerated. In contrast, skilled, conscientious employees threaten incompetent bullies because they are more likely to challenge bad decisions, justifiably react to inappropriate behaviours or defend their professional reputation when criticised. Consequently, they make better bully fodder. Sadly, when the bullying game begins, even capable employees can become less competent.

Bullies may have good job skills, but lack competence in relating to other employees. Many lack the social and emotional intelligence to feel empathy for another person's feelings or show compassion. They don't use appropriate social skills, such as communication skills or absorb feedback.[12] They bully instead of developing relationships with other employees. However, as no-one likes being labelled a bully, they will deny it.

> 'My employers felt they were entitled to do whatever they liked, as they'd been making decisions without any accountability for decades. They promoted incompetent teachers out of the classroom, while leaving the competent ones to teach but still managed by those with poor skills and respect for teaching. They maintained a vicious determination to ensure everyone who 'shone' belonged to the dominant clique; the actual work was irrelevant, and work performance wasn't even on the radar. As I excelled at teaching, and wasn't in the clique, the rest is history.

> *The CEO who could have prevented my bullying before it esca-*
> *lated bluntly told me that my ability would mean I was a threat.'*

Some managers are quick, cunning thinkers but poor at implementation and organisation; for example, in relation to time management, investigations, and budgets. They lack patience and persistence, and ignore feedback. Some lack motivation to work hard but seek recognition, status and power to compensate for something they desire. Adversarial managers target scapegoats to avoid confronting underlying problems and resolving them respectfully. According to the hierarchy of needs theory postulated by the American psychologist Abraham Maslow, they have achieved their basic physiological needs but little else.[13] They are insecure and frustrated, and some may be depressed. They appear arrogant and patronising, unable to respect themselves or others. Consequently, they are threatened by conscientious employees and high achievers, and do not want to employ anyone better than themselves. Ordinary bullies do not realise that they achieve far more by being respectful and inclusive, instead of using divisive, destructive power games.

When bullies are rewarded, promoted or given a great reference to move on — while their targets are disciplined, demoted or outed — then mediocrity is fostered. Other employees learn to support the bully to maintain their job, while those who confront or challenge the bully face dismissal. Witnesses are manipulated or abandoned to cope on their own so that everyone learns to mind their own business, not the company's goals. Eventually, the incompetent bully stays and the competent target moves on or breaks down. As most workplaces depend upon employee performance, together with effective interpersonal skills, bullies have defective work skills which negatively impact upon everything they do, reducing the quality of their work and others. Thus bullying hides performance and interpersonal incompetence.

Reduced motivation

> *'I was expected to maintain a professional image for clients. But*
> *following his bullying, it was impossible to hide my tears, and my*
> *makeup would smudge.'*

Bullying sabotages an employee's commitment to work. It undermines performance, stifles creativity and reduces productivity. When employees cannot connect with one another, they feel excluded and insignificant; this lowers staff morale and motivation, and is followed by concentration

---

Are there signs of bullying at your workplace?

• Higher absenteeism rates

• Sudden changes in punctuality

• Unexpected resignations

• Increased work conflict

• Unexplained increase in emotional outbursts

• Toxic work culture

• Decrease in productivity

• Increased mistakes

• Avoidable physical injuries

• Increased fraud, malpractice, or unethical behaviours

• Increased reports of drug and alcohol abuse

• Increased grievance processes and litigation

• Increased workers compensation or personal injury claims

• Employee sabotage

---

difficulties. Many feel threatened and experience mood changes, such as becoming tearful, angry, moody, stressed or withdrawn. This increases absenteeism and sick leave. Other employees are then expected to fill these jobs and increase their workload. The result is increased levels of non-compliance with company procedures, less respect for guidelines, poor execution of orders, an increase in mistakes and more attempts at sabotage.

A climate of fear and intimidation stops workmates supporting their friends and erodes the communication between employees and the public, sponsoring poor public relations. There are higher rates of staff turnover, sudden resignations, unexpected requests for transfers, retirements due to ill-health and absences resulting from long service leave. If the bully blackens a target's reputation for years or refuses to provide a reference, the target is stopped from leaving and obtaining another job. Their frustration is reflected in their reduced work output or by subtle sabotage, which has a destructive influence on the work environment and teamwork.

Mismanagement and fraud

> *'When I complained about poor safety standards, I was accused of having personal relationship difficulties and bullied out for whistleblowing.'*

> *'He said, "Make the figures up by tomorrow". If you challenged him you got punished. I call him "the eliminator".'*

Bullying can disguise fraud, malpractice or expensive mistakes as managers build their career without respecting their company's best interests or ethical responsibilities. Although many employees are hired for their professional expertise, they are forced to agree with the bully, despite their professional opposition. Sometimes bullying creates a fear of reporting mistakes, leading to strategic disasters. Gary Collis, Employee Ombudsman in the South Australian government, notes that 'Errors, sometimes costing millions of dollars, frequently result from the victim not being given information or having key documents removed from his desk or computer'.[14]

Brain drain

> *'We have a staff turnover like autumn leaves.'*

When people with expertise and experience are bullied out of their jobs, the organisation loses a bank of knowledge and professional support built over many years. Highly skilled witnesses may also leave when possible. Brilliance, creativity, good customer relations, and years of practical experience all go unrewarded. The loss of these skills may be difficult to replace in the corporate memory and staff support structure. An organisation's reputation for bullying deters future high-quality employees and attracts those with poorer skills, thereby increasing staff replacement and training costs.

Some statistics

- 85% of bullies have bullied before, 34% of new supervisors bully, 25% of targets leave, 20% of witnesses leave.[15]
- 40% of targets never report the bullying, 3% sue and 4% complain to state or federal agencies.[16]
- Bullied employees waste between 10% and 52% of their time at work protecting themselves, obtaining support, and feeling stressed and demotivated.[17]
- Managers spend 40% of their time managing employee conflicts.[18]

- 58% of women report experiencing harassing behaviours at work.[19]
- The Center for Disease Control in the United States reports that 15 murders occur each week in the workplace, making it the third largest cause of death on the job. For women, it is the primary cause of death at work. Also one in four US workers reported being harassed, threatened or attacked on the job in a 1-year period.[20]
- It costs on average between 50% and 150% of a person's salary to replace them.[21]
- Every day in the United States, nearly one million employees miss work because of workplace stress.[22]

The financial cost of bullying

> *'I saved a large corporation $5.7 million when I reduced the bullying.'*

The costs of bullying vary around the world due to many factors, such as different cultures, types of legal compensation and procedures. Research is affected by different types of analysis. Sometimes bullying statistics are identified separately or hidden within harassment, discrimination, stress and violence statistics. However, bullying costs modern society billions of dollars annually.

- The Australian Productivity Commission estimates bullying and harassment costs the economy about $14.8 billion a year.[23]
- Workplace stress costs the United States economy US$300 billion in absenteeism, employee turnover, lost productivity and medical, legal and insurance costs, which equates to $7,600 per employee per year.[24]
- A single episode of workplace violence can cost $250,000 in lost time and legal expenses.[25]
- Litigation settlements in the United States have reached over US$2 million.[26]
- Bullying cost a New Zealand company NZ$500,000+ due to staff turnover, absenteeism, lowered productivity, mistakes, conflict and litigation.[27]
- It has been calculated that between 0.5–3.5% of a nation's GDP may be spent on the outcomes of stress and violence at work.[28]

Employee payouts
- A British teacher was sacked for misconduct and later awarded £230,000 following long-term bullying by his former principal.

- An Australian victim of workplace bullying was awarded more than $515,000 after his employer failed to follow its own statement of values and culture.
- A woman in Massachusetts was awarded US$730,000 from her company for bullying and retaliation.
- A Fiji-born man from Sydney was awarded $1.9 million following years of physical, verbal and racial bullying.
- Christina Rich, the highest-paid female employee at Pricewaterhouse Coopers, was awarded several million dollars for damage to her reputation, loss of clients, lost earnings and counselling after a series of alleged sexual harassment and bullying incidents from 1999 to 2004.

Yet even these costs may underestimate the problem. According to the Workplace Bullying Project Team at Griffith University, Australia,[29] the full impact of workplace bullying could cost up to $36 billion per year. Of course, all of these cost estimates are limited to the business sector. They do not include costs to family, health and personal life, the cost of divorce and associated family services, the government or privately run medical benefits systems, or unemployment benefits — as well as the impact on the wider community. Clearly, the cost of not dealing with bullying in a constructive way is extremely high.

There is a growing expectation of organisations to respect their social responsibilities; slowly they are being made more accountable for child labour, pollution, deforestation, water conservation and inappropriate mining. They are being encouraged to create a better work–life balance to maintain families and communities.

Thus, if an organisation needs to build its social capital and maintain its duty of care, then auditors, accountants and human resources departments should maintain regular financial audits of bullying to investigate any destructive impact upon their production of goods or services.

The organisational costs of bullying

Obvious costs

- *Absenteeism*
- *Increased rates of sick leave and temporary replacement costs*
- *Turnover and replacement costs, including advertising, interviewing, selection, training; administration costs; impact of low staffing levels or temporary replacement staff; time for new staff to become fully functioning*
- *Investigations, mediation, dispute resolution and grievance procedures costs*
- *Psychological, psychiatric, medical treatment and insurance costs*
- *Costs associated with obtaining legal expertise to negotiate a variety of claims*
- *Costs associated with fines and payouts to victims such as superannuation, wage entitlements, long service leave, vicarious liability*
- *Higher insurance premiums*

Hidden costs

- *Reduced productivity during and after the bullying, leading to organisational inertia*
- *Lowered motivation, workforce commitment and morale*
- *Increased likelihood of mistakes, mismanagement, fraud and unethical standards*
- *Backlash, sabotage or payback by targets, bullies, and witnesses*
- *Time lost by employees to protect themselves, obtain help, debrief, prepare for legal cases*
- *Costs associated with disciplinary action (e.g., meetings, administration), including professional costs for HR consultants and lawyers*
- *Extra office administration costs to deal with disputes and all legal actions*
- *Impact of media and other adverse publicity leading to poor public relations and loss of brand equity*
- *Loss of good employees, mentors and managers and increased likelihood of attracting less competent one*

From target to survivor

❝*When I started working at the Bully Fest 2000 [my metaphor for my new workplace] the method of socialising was zinger-flinging. At lunchbreaks the 'girl clique' liked to hurl insults. If your insult was particularly witty you sometimes got '10,000 Zinger Points'. I felt uncomfortable and let people know (after several painful and anxious occasions). They said I was too sensitive and was making a big deal out of nothing, but I noticed people trying to cover up hurt feelings during and after the 'zinging'. What struck me most is that people loved to dish it out and hated to take it — almost without exception. When I had had enough of the zinging insults and walked out of the room, I was known for 'storming out', which became the next big joke. I had to put up with the junior bully making snide remarks, followed by 'I'm just kidding'.*❞

Who can be targeted?

Any dog lover knows that a dog with one flea can scratch all day, while another dog, riddled with fleas, won't react. Although organisations are responsible for reducing bullying, not everyone is targeted or injured. The same triggers may hardly affect one person, energise another to take action, and traumatise someone else. There are many reasons why you can become a target.

Bullying may begin when:
- your excellent performance exposes someone else's incompetence
- something about you makes someone else jealous
- you are different to others
- the previous target of a bully leaves
- you support a colleague who's being bullied
- you gain a new, inexperienced and pressured manager

- you whistleblow about difficulties, for example, incompetence, malpractice
- you refuse to violate company guidelines
- you challenge the bullying behaviour instead of confronting or blocking it
- a blind spot leads you to become unaware of others' vulnerabilities and mistakes — this can make you appear patronising, provocative or punitive
- you are unassertive and try to avoid conflict
- you are handicapped by other life stressors and ignore danger signs.

How do you become a target?

> *Nina was a conscientious, respected welfare worker. Suddenly she was ostracised, devalued, excluded. It was a real shock. She regarded her downfall as a slide from valued to devalued. Since her exit, she found 13 other employees who were bullied out. Former work colleagues were forbidden to speak to her. Her claim for workers compensation was initially rejected by her employer but she won, three years later.*

You become a target of bullying when you experience insults, emotional abuse and other bullying behaviours. Many people, however, regard bullying as an employment hazard, such is the prevalence of aggressive management styles in today's workplace. They simply press their reset

button and move on. However, others become injured, yet the injury isn't viewed in the same way as a physical injury.

Just imagine that a worker slipped on a banana peel in the corridor at their office. If they were young and healthy they might quickly regain their balance, suffering only a sprain, and mutter something about careless people while limping back to their desk. If they were an older person they may not recover their balance as quickly, fall heavily, and may be badly bruised or even break a bone. In either case they would not be blamed for stepping on the banana peel, slipping and sustaining injuries. It would be considered an unfortunate accident; they were in the wrong place at the wrong time. Colleagues would be sympathetic — maybe sending get-well notes, balloons or flowers.

Alternatively, imagine a bank teller suffering a hold-up. Someone jabs a long, pointed object in their neck and growls in a muffled voice to drop to the floor. Most people would be affected by the event, becoming upset and emotional straight afterwards. Depending on their personalities and life experiences some would recover relatively quickly, while others would be traumatised for ages. Even if the object was found to be a harmless plastic toy, the law would still consider the person a victim of a serious crime. The police would validate the victim's statements about the trauma they felt by having had a 'gun' pointed at them. A critical incident team might descend on the workplace to debrief everyone and try to ensure that the fallout effects are limited. There would be no devaluing of the victim for being traumatised by such an event. Support would be offered and they would slowly resume their life.

Tragically, the picture is drastically different in the case of workplace bullying. You are not treated the same as the recipient of a work accident or a critical incident when you suffer injuries at work from unsuccessfully dealing with bullying. In fact, you are likely to not even be recognised as being injured. This lack of acknowledgment can turn a target of workplace bullying into a victim. Then you can experience even more injury when you are forced out of work and handicapped by adversarial, medico–legal systems. You may watch your bully, managers, colleagues, insurer and medico–legal professionals grow wealthier, while your financial situation withers. Simultaneously, everything else in your life suffers.

Thus, although nearly anyone can be targeted for bullying, there is no current evidence proving your increased vulnerability to becoming a victim. Research only demonstrates how bullying can injure you. There are no valid *before and after* personality tests. Like predicting a potential murder victim, it is impossible to obtain an accurate victim profile. Trauma is regarded as distressing to any normal person. Apart from your personal, social and employment history, it is impossible for a doctor, psychologist, psychiatrist or lawyer to accurately assess your personality before you were bullied. The only exceptions are employees who have experienced earlier trauma, workplace bullying or school bullying, which increases their vulnerability, although the symptoms of school bullying and other traumas are different.

Generally, school bullying targets obtain some sympathy. In countries such as Australia and the United States you are more likely to be blamed and shamed for declaring yourself a victim of workplace bullying. Thus you become a *victim* when you are deeply injured by the accumulation of sustained bullying behaviours, the social and professional humiliation, and your organisation's continuing battle to blame you and deny you natural justice. When you perceive this whole experience as humiliating, destructive and traumatic, you can be changed forever and seriously injured, just like other victims of long-term abuse.

The journey: From target to survivor

Over a lifetime of psychological practice I have watched many different psychological theories materialise. Some are extremely valuable and practical; some are misrepresented or overestimated, while others inflict arrogant damage, which is later refuted. The notion of arranging varied and complex experiences into a concept of stages is professionally challenging. The workplace bullying support groups I have been involved with over many years have allowed for the careful mapping out of what I believe are seven stages towards survival. You may hardly notice some stages whereas others will be re-experienced and revisited in many different ways. At any stage you can feel very angry, scared or sad. Your journey, including every stage, may take months or many years. You life is on hold, like a plane on the tarmac. Ultimately, you need some kind of *internal* (from yourself) or *external* (from the public) *validation* to move on.

Stage 1: The initial impact — identify the bullying behaviours

> Sarah worked successfully for years on a medical research project. When the new nurse manager arrived, with her reputation as a bully, they shared a tiny, cramped office. She would lecture Sarah, yell, exclude her from duties, withhold messages, and undermine the research project. 'You're not a team member,' she said. Sarah's concentration was affected, she had sleep difficulties and a car accident.

In stage 1 you identify at a conscious or unconscious level that something is very wrong. You are not sure what is happening, but you realise that these behaviours are not fair or justified although some may be so subtle and insidious that they take months or years to reach a crisis point. You may or may not identify them as bullying or yourself as a target. Your experiences include shock, confusion, unreality, denial, fear, shame, guilt, self-blame, anger, defensiveness, hope and physical sickness. You look for other ways to cope — for example, by drinking and overeating.

You might react in the following ways:

- With shock, confusion, or a sense of unreality: *Am I being bullied? I can't believe this is happening to me. I'm getting sick of going to work.*
- By denying there is anything wrong: *They don't mean to hurt me. I can cope, I survived an abusive marriage. There are other things I need to focus on at work.*

Confronting the obstacle

- By trivialising the issue: *It doesn't really matter. It isn't really that bad. It's not severe enough to make a complaint.*
- By hoping that the situation will change: *It'll improve eventually. Once they have disciplined me it will stop. Something will change.*
- By self-blaming: *I've done something wrong. I made a minor mistake. I could have done more. I shouldn't have let this happen.*

Action plan

Listen to your gut instinct, get professional help, consider your options, devise coping strategies, confront or exit. Don't leave it to chance to improve on its own.

Stage 2: The unsuccessful attempt to stop the bullying

> Cherie complained to the HR department and they organised five meetings with her manager. At no stage was the bullying ever discussed. They changed the game to focus on her job description and threatened some disciplinary procedures. The union representative remained silent. Not long after her breakdown, the bully was sacked!

Although you confront the bully and/or your manager, they deny, minimise, condone, retaliate or lack procedures to stop the bullying. Perhaps they think that bullying is harmless, or improves productivity, or they don't know how to manage bullying effectively. Others, including your union, the human resources staff, and senior management may also blame you or sabotage you as a way of avoiding their responsibilities. Your colleagues quickly forget all the good things you did for them and the good times they shared with you. They become evasive, and abandon or betray you. Suddenly you are totally alone and derailed: nobody at work cares about you, nobody understands that all you need is acknowledgment or validation of feeling bullied (your perception) and a *safe workplace*.

You might have the following responses:

- A sense of injustice: *We have a no-bullying policy, they should stop it. Why are they attacking me, I've done nothing wrong?*
- Feeling fearful and powerless: *What will happen next? I don't want to lose my job. There's nothing I can do.*
- Feeling angry: *How dare they treat me like this! No one will help me.*

Action plan

Be warned that bullying can affect everything else in your life as well as this job. You alone are responsible for your health and wellbeing. Once your organisation condones, denies or becomes adversarial, you cannot expect them to help. You need to take action to protect yourself and avoid injury. Use your survival instinct to fight or flee.

Feeling stuck, unable to move

Stage 3: Powerlessness and paralysis

> *'The third stage was clear to me when I no longer had control over my body, I had diarrhoea, was dry-retching, my throat was constantly tight, I was constantly teary, couldn't sleep, couldn't function and lost my normal coping mechanisms. I kept working for six months while my symptoms deteriorated, then I was too sick to resign.'*

Despite your endeavours, nothing you do seems to make a difference. The external message is so different to your own perception, that it feels like a hypnotic trance and splits your identity. You may feel over-whelmed, powerless to control yourself or your environment, forced to submit, stuck in time and space. You may disassociate to survive and exist in a numb, zombie, or robotic-like state. It is akin to experiencing a sneaking, creeping emotional and physical paralysis as you lose control.

You may experience high blood pressure, depression or panic attacks. You cannot concentrate, speak or write clearly. You stop working efficiently and can hardly cope with basic chores. Like other victims of sustained, chronic trauma, you experience intense fear, help-lessness, shock or horror.

You begin to say things such as:

- *I remember just waking up — everything seemed unreal, I was unravel-ling, no longer a living, feeling person. I was totally numb, operating on automatic.*
- *There was a slow build-up, I had to submit and go through the whole thing, there was nothing I could do and no circuit-breaker.*
- *It's an out-of-body experience. I'm fighting a brick wall. I'm caught in a whirlpool.*

Action plan

When dealing with powerlessness you need to release your fear and anger otherwise your survival instinct will remain stuck. Try to move constantly between your past, present and future. Look after yourself and obtain support from professionals, family and friends.

Things look even worse

Stage 4: The search for validation and justice

*Lena spent 8 angry, teary months on workers insurance.
She found it hard to get up in the morning and put on a happy
facade for her family. Her career was shattered and the consequences reverberated through her everyday existence. She hated
the local community gossip surrounding her departure. She felt a
failure, and despite being traumatised, accepted a similar job to
prove that she was still competent and worthwhile. She went
from the frying pan into the fire. The bullying was as bad as it
had been at her previous job. Although she didn't take the
bullying personally, the damage to her emotional health was
cumulative. Two years later she was battling cancer.*

By stage 4 your life has been badly affected in many different ways. Your
self-esteem may be shattered and you may feel angry that you are disempowered and traumatised, especially as you believed yourself to be a
diligent, competent employee — otherwise you would have been sacked
ages ago. Although you may have been criticised towards the end, there
was no previous warning of their 'concerns'. Besides, even if you had made
some mistakes, you did not deserve to be bullied. Slowly, you investigate
the bully's role and your organisation's betrayal to find out why you were
bullied and subsequently injured. Ultimately, you need to obtain some
private and public *validation* to prove that you were bullied.

Like victims of war, rape or criminal assault, you seek *justice* to punish
the bullies and your employer, who ignored your request for validation
and safety. Legal action can provide some justice, vindication, validation
and financial compensation for what you have suffered and lost. However,

legal actions take years to be explored, resolved or abandoned. You are in limbo until they are resolved. Unfortunately, your recovery is paralysed until you experience some form of validation.

You say things such as:

- *I want to restore my good name.*
- *I did nothing wrong, why should I lose the job I loved?*
- *I know about bullying now and want to stop it happening to others.*

Action plan

Try to find alternative ways to achieve validation or obtain justice. Friends, family, therapists and workplace bullying support groups can provide validation and support. Knowing others were also bullied or that the bully was disciplined after you left will help. An expert lawyer will advise you on your legal options.

Stage 5: Coping with your injuries

> *Once Jack was forced to stay home he realised how he sick he was. He had put on weight and had high blood pressure. He suffered insomnia, depression and high levels of anger and fear. His self-esteem had taken a real battering. His family and social life were affected and he went out. He felt like a hamster in a wheel as he faced the grindstone every day, with no relief or joy in life.*

Stage 5 starts with the truth striking home — you have been injured by the bullying. You continue to experience painful and debilitating feelings such as hopelessness, shame and humiliation. Your self-esteem and work identity may feel shattered, your spirit broken. Because you need all your energies to cope and survive, you cannot do many things at once. You may neglect ordinary duties like your home, personal grooming or paperwork. You eat poorly, stop exercising regularly and avoid recreational activities. You may avoid extended family and socialising with friends as you find it hard to explain to them what you are going through. You change from being socially active to becoming socially handicapped.

Slowly you become aware of the clinical symptoms that can seriously affect your emotional health. Because you could not stop the bullying when it was happening, you compensate by obsessing for years about every detail associated with the bullying and its impact on your life. This validates your experiences and helps you understand what happened.

You may develop a hypervigilant or paranoid fear and find it hard to feel safe anywhere except at home, regarding even telephone calls as threatening. Minor situations, such as leaving the safety of home for a medical appointment or going to the supermarket, take on the guise of a major danger and can trigger a panic attack. You become suspicious and uncomfortable around strangers; for example, on public transport, in shopping malls, at movies, or in church. Certain objects, such as a car that looks like the bully's car, can bring back difficult memories. Painful memories may trigger latent symptoms of an earlier traumatic event, such as bullying by a step-parent.

You say things such as:

- *My body has broken down. I'm not the same person anymore.*
- *I lock myself inside, leave the curtains drawn and do a doona dive.*
- *My friends are sick of hearing about the bullying, they can't believe it hasn't been resolved.*

Action plan

You need to identify your injuries and obtain the appropriate treatment to heal. You will need to confront painful thoughts and feelings, while caring for yourself physically and emotionally. Use your extended support network, especially while dealing with any medico–legal processes.

Stage 6: Mourning your losses

> Sally had retrained later in life. Despite the bullies, she enjoyed working with colleagues and helping clients. She mourned the loss of her job, the fun she'd shared with workmates, and the fact that she'd never work in this career again.

Like many victims, you have two choices: accept that your bullying experience was not fair and create a new life, or spend the rest of your days moaning about the lack of justice. You know that bad things happen to good people all the time and that real justice is unattainable. Although you did not deserve to be injured, it happened; it changed your life and you need time to heal. Thus you need to *mourn* the temporary or permanent losses to your mental and physical health, personality, career, financial status, family, sex life, social relationships and anything else. There may be spiritual losses, such as your loss of innocence about your ability to cope, or your lost belief about the world being a good place. Sometimes there is a trigger such as the end of a court case, or something nice like a better job, that helps the mourning process.

If you blamed yourself, then this is the time to forgive yourself, although you may want to do this gradually. You may even wish to forgive those who bullied you because of the toxic work culture. If you cannot forgive, then release your anger; do not keep it inside, otherwise it will fester and poison your emotional system. Once you have mourned your losses, you will find some closure.

You say things like:

- *It was the perfect job for me, I won't find one like that again.*
- *I'm sad I couldn't be a good mother while it was happening.*
- *Maybe I should leave my blinds up during the day.*

Action plan

You may wish to find meaningful rituals to mourn your losses and signify a symbolic closure — for example, meditate with incense and candles, burn an effigy of the bully, organise a special ceremony (like an Irish wake), throw out your previous work-clothes, and give feedback about your experiences to management and others.

Stage 7: Becoming a survivor

> *Vicki was trained from childhood to put her family, friends and others first. She was a classic obliging provider! Once the illness and court cases were over, she found a lovely job with better pay. She vowed never to let anyone bully her again. She has begun to value, protect and pamper herself and is determined to enjoy life.*

Although Sleeping Beauty was woken with a kiss from the handsome prince, no one wakes you up from years of pain and trauma. The moment you start making the best of a rotten situation you become a *survivor*. Any minor form of acknowledgment or validation accelerates your recovery. You cannot return to the past, but must accept change and move on. Survival means rebirth and restoration. Like the survivors of war crimes, you need to reconstruct and recreate a life for yourself.

Just like Humpty Dumpty, you need to put your life back together again, piece by piece. You start this process by making lots of new beginnings. You will find many minuscule turning points that signpost your long road to recovery, and although you will make plans, be flexible and update when necessary. This slow process of recovery involves rebuilding your physical and emotional health, self-esteem, career and social life. There will be good moments and bad moments, a few steps forward and a few back. Slowly you will find that you can do more and more each day. The bad times eventually fade.

Eventually you may understand the significance of your experience. Maybe the universe wanted you to discover new beliefs, inner wisdom and values to improve life for everyone else, as well as protect your own health and wellbeing. This could include the power to listen to your intuition, trust your gut feelings and value yourself more deeply. You may become more aware of the fragility of life and value every moment. You may become less tolerant of superficial people or trivial issues, and seek more satisfying relationships or situations. Perhaps your bullying experience will make it easier for others to obtain validation or help you battle against injustice.

You say things like:

- *Now I can go to the supermarket on my own.*
- *I have more frequent moments where I feel calm.*
- *I can't forget, but I've moved on and am getting on with life.*

Action plan

You begin by re-establishing everyday routines and behaviours, such as answering the phone instantly, keeping your home tidy, reading your mail, losing weight. It could help to do things differently. You may begin looking for a new career or rewarding ways to spend your time, such as hobbies or voluntary work. It is important to learn assertive skills to confront bullies — they may be working at other places too!

Slowly you reconstruct your self-confidence and nurture your shattered self-esteem. It helps to use caring support and feedback from others. Try to identify the signs that symbolise your move from target to survivor, such as power dressing, strong eye contact, clear speech.

One day, you may be sitting alone quietly, writing or chatting with others, when you reflect upon what it meant to be bullied and how it changed your life. You will find pain, such as losing your job and old friends, but there will be gains such as your improved assertive skills. Thus you can use your insights to understand the impact of the workplace bullying on your life and build your emotional and social resilience.

The value of the stages

> Betty used the stages as a warning sign to take action. She was being bullied in her next job and beginning to react in self-harming ways. She identified her pain and realised that she was in danger. This time she complained immediately instead of ignoring it. 'I know where I am and I know where I am going next.'

The stages can help you express your distress and validate your experiences. They demonstrate that others experience bullying in a similar manner. Clearly, you are not alone. You can use the stages to understand what went wrong, what you are experiencing now and what you need to do to recover and heal, such as finding some external validation. Then plan your options and take action.

One survivor's story

'The whole bullying experience has left me with some personal developments I couldn't have expected. I'm alive — every moment — I feel life within me and around me. Before … I was asleep. Recovering from an attempted suicide means I now value every moment I have. "Life is beautiful", and anything that happens to me now could never be as painful as those two years of hell. I'm more open now — less fearful — and I feel all the beauty and suffering of the world acutely. I'm so fortunate to benefit from this wisdom! I don't wish anyone to be bullied but now I see the experience as a precious gift. I could take the road of lasting bitterness and anger but I choose to use my pain for my own personal and spiritual development. Now, as a result of all that suffering, I want to do more to alleviate it in others. I'm going to be a nurse. I don't think I would have found that path if I wasn't bullied. I certainly would not have the compassion I do now. Thank you, bullies, you've helped me find my true calling.'

Relevance for employers

These stages have significant implications for improving productivity in a workplace. Their core message means that it is far more ethical and economical to validate targets' perceptions immediately, provide them with a safe working environment or make them redundant than bully them out. The collaborative approach, which utilises respectful resolutions to resolving differences, is far more constructive than the adversarial approach, in which employers condone bullying and condemn some employees, and where everyone — employers, employees, consumers and the work culture — loses.

Relevance for mental health professionals

Diagnosing and treating victims of workplace bullying is a very new area and lacks comprehensive, evidence-based research. Targets may require access to a variety of treatment options from numerous mental health professionals. Clearly, learning social survival skills or resilience to block bullying is simple and useful before the target is injured. Once an employee has been injured, then different approaches are required as the injuries may be extensive and life-threatening. They can use the journey from target to survivor to identify the most appropriate stages to describe the target or victim, understand why many find it difficult to adjust to their changed circumstances, and heal and move on, despite having left their toxic workplace. The stages can assist health practitioners to provide a more accurate, up-to-date diagnosis and develop more relevant stage-appropriate treatment plans.

I believe the need for validation is the key to understanding the level of injury and treatment required in cases of workplace bullying. Thus, providing an injured victim with brief, 'cost-effective' therapies like cognitive–behaviour therapy, when their validating court cases or next job loom years ahead and they require long-term psychological support, may be insufficient therapeutically and possibly negligent ethically. Eventually, the stages may enable insurance companies, rehabilitation consultants and other medico–legal systems to provide victims with more effective treatments.

Activate your survival instinct

> ❝ *'I had a life damn you, I had a life' is a quote from the movie Ghost. It reverberates around my mind. I too had a life before the bullying, although I couldn't say when I actually lost it. It seemed so gradual. It took a close friend to finally sit me down and ask, 'When did you eat last? When did you sleep? Are you walking the dogs? Are you getting out of the house?' I had no idea of the answers. I was hardly existing. I lost contact with my upbeat friends because all I felt was doom and gloom. The ever-wide circle of my life was diminishing down to a standstill. Through it all my dogs were my support. I'd laugh with my dogs. Smile at their antics. They are my reason to get out of bed so that I can walk them. Yet in my depths of despair I couldn't decide which dog path to take. So I would stand and just cry, unable to make this simple decision. Eventually I put one foot in front of the other. Going to my church was impor-tant; I'd scurry in and try to hide from people. I could not make small talk. I often put my hand up for prayer though my faith has crumbled at times, but it keeps me going. Surviving? Yes, still. Living? Occasionally. Enjoying Life? Maybe one day. Having a life? It will never be the same and maybe hopefully it will be a different kind of something.* ❞

The core issue when faced with a trauma or tragedy is not what happened, but how you can understand, protect yourself, endure the distressing challenges, release your pain, heal and move on. You were born with a survival instinct. This essential fight or flight instinct energises you to take action and transforms your anger or fear into a biochemical power that can protect you.

If you feel that you are between a rock and a hard place, then you need to activate, reinvigorate, reinstate, reinvent or unlock your survival instinct. You cannot afford to do nothing and wait for others to intervene because you will become powerless and paralysed. That is when the major psychological and physical injury occurs.

People experience untold horrors by other humans, from childhood sexual abuse to the tortures of war. Some find it impossible to forget or focus upon other matters, whereas others constantly confront their pain and move on, creating a different life. Although their emotional and physical scars are permanent, they are survivors.

The fact is that anyone can be targeted and injured by workplace bullying, but it is not a permanent label. How you deal with your experience is up to you. Once you change your attitude and actions, you can regard this as another example of life's challenges that need to be confronted, and automatically you become a survivor.

How do people survive?

The well-known psychiatrist Viktor Frankl survived a concentration camp and finished his best selling book *Man's Search For Meaning* six weeks after being released.[1] He believes that humans are ultimately self-determining. They can choose to survive shocking situations provided their will or belief is strong. They also have the potential to be decent or evil, or in other words, 'to be nice or not nice', as he once told me.

Most stories of survivors share a common thread. They find something very powerful inside their soul to inspire resilience, maintain their fighting

spirit and pursue their drive to survive. Even when survival seems highly improbable, as for the buried survivors of a mine collapse, the human body has an amazing capacity to endure and function. Survivors focus on what they can do, instead of obsessing about what's no longer possible.

Turn a life-threatening experience into a life-altering experience

Don't sacrifice your health for a job. No job is worth your life.[2]

Most people work to live, they don't live to work. Thus, although you may find yourself in an intolerable work situation that you cannot change right now, you only become a victim if you believe that you are completely powerless or regard the bullying as life-threatening. Your prime focus is to protect yourself, not the pursuit of justice or associated goals. You may need to regard bullying as one of life's more difficult challenges, because once you reframe the bullying, you become a survivor. Then you can regard it as a life-altering but complex experience.

Challenge the rules

> *The 60-year-old woman was asleep in her tent when she heard the young man scream. He was being dragged towards the river by a saltwater crocodile. She ran and jumped on the animal's back. The crocodile became distracted, dropped its prey, turned to attack her and was shot dead by her son.*

Survivors of war, natural disasters, poverty and other disasters are often forced to reassess the rules by which they live. This means that sometimes these rules have to be rejected, discarded, distorted or eliminated. Survival becomes the key focus. It is like reprogramming your mind, or fixing a system malfunction. This means becoming more flexible in your thinking and using whatever tools are necessary for your survival. You empower yourself by playing survival games.

Investigate all options

> *Jack Kilby failed to gain entrance to the prestigious Massachusetts Institute of Technology. Thus he was extremely aware of what he didn't know. Consequently, for the rest of his research career he tended to investigate as many options to a problem as possible. His persistence won him a Nobel Prize and helped create the microchip, transforming our world.*

Each person will experience bullying differently, as everyone comes from a different perspective and background. You need to be creative and innovative when dealing with your problems because things are not always what they seem at first. Just as an author can spend ages mulling over one word, spend time considering all the angles. Instead of automatically slotting yourself into the role of powerless target, you may find another way to approach the situation, such as finding out what else is going on for managers, bullies and onlookers at work. Maybe your situation will look different and, hopefully, offer more constructive solutions.

Explore your options and consult your support network for advice and feedback. Find out how far up the organisation ladder you can go for help; there is not much stopping you going right to the top, beyond middle management when necessary. Go back to them repeatedly if their instructions to middle managers fail. Your best option is to consult your organisation but, if they deny your request for respect and justice, be prepared to challenge or leave. If leaving is impractical, then go into self-protection mode to survive, block out the toxic atmosphere, and reprogram yourself to confront any future threats or challenges.

Use your survival instinct

When our forebears lived in jungles, they used their survival (*fight/flight*) instinct to assess the appropriate action to take. Today, you need to work out your best options in the work jungle. Your first inclination may be to fight, not with a club, but to use your resources to be assertive and proactive, and confront the issue. Another option is to take flight, which involves moving away, playing games or leaving. You can aim for validation and justice later on.

However, if there is no other option you can freeze and do nothing; not because you are powerless but because that is what is appropriate, in the same way as you might when you confront a grizzly bear until he moves away. You need to remain cool and not reveal any emotional intensity, otherwise you will threaten the bully and his support team, who will retaliate.

Avoid recriminations

Although you may now believe that you should have fled the bullying, at the time you thought your actions were secure. Perhaps other factors made you become more vulnerable, such as your age, no support or poor employment opportunities. Do not blame yourself for being in the wrong place at the wrong time. You would have been fine somewhere else and hopefully you will eventually move to somewhere else that suits you better.

Discard old values

Many people hoard food, clothes and linen in their cupboards for years after their use-by date. Check your mental closet and trash shabby or faulty myths/beliefs about equity and justice that don't apply to your toxic workplace:

- *I'm nice to them, they should be nice to me.*
- *I can handle a toxic workplace.*
- *I'm entitled to respect, justice and a fair deal.*
- *I did nothing wrong, why should I change?*
- *There should be genuine justice for injured workers.*
- *This isn't a jungle.*

Are you an ordinary hero?

When you think about heroes, names like Mandela and Gandhi come to mind. However, everyday people can become ordinary heroes and confront evils like bullying, even while others remain silent. If you decide to confront the bullying, your path will be challenging and difficult like the hero's journey in Joseph Campbell's book, *The Hero with a Thousand Faces.*[3] Along the way you will find special mentors and eventually you will be transformed by your experiences and make the world a safer place.

Beware that the solitary hero is more likely to be shamed and blamed. You are more effective when you operate within a social network. Thus whistleblowers, targets and witnesses need to be supported by three or more people to be respected by employers, unions and lawyers.

Consider the options for change

Your workplace needs to change if there is bullying, while you need to find skills to empower yourself. Your emotional survival will depend on how well you assess your options for change.

Option 1: No one changes

You've done nothing wrong so you do nothing. Your organisation condones bullying and gets away with it.

Possible outcome: *You suffer. You and others may leave. Bullies continue. Both you and the organisation lose.*

Option 2: The organisation changes

Following a bullying event, they improve procedures with dispute resolution processes that are respectful and fair. You are affected if you do not obtain healing and learn how to protect yourself.

Possible outcome: *You are injured by the bullying. If you leave you may be still affected or bullied elsewhere. You lose, the organisation wins.*

Option 3: You change

Regardless of what your organisation does, you need to take appropriate action to protect yourself, otherwise your health and career will be affected.

Possible outcome: *The organisation does nothing, you develop self-protective strategies. You win, the organisation loses.*

Option 4: You and the organisation change

You become a survivor and your company becomes ethically, legally, socially and financially responsible. They respect and train every employee to maintain a safe, productive workplace.

Possible outcome: *You and the organisation benefit, a real win–win situation.*

Make the big switch — recycle pain into power

Resilience means adapting to the ups and downs of life regardless of justice or equity. It means assessing your options, taking action and improving these processes. Listen to others and utilise their feedback.

- *Learn what is reasonable:* If everyone is under pressure at work then your manager may be stressed. If you appear oversensitive and overreact, colleagues will not be supportive, so use their feedback as a guide.

- *Don't be fooled:* Assess their feedback when you confront your organisation. Do they value you and your work? Will they take appropriate steps to validate your concerns and provide a safe working environment? If not, stop pretending they care and start protecting yourself.

- *Build boundaries:* If you are not valued, then fulfil your basic, mandatory work requirements; do not just work harder to please a malicious bully. If you work in crocodile territory, avoid approaching or antagonising them.

- *Don't go ballistic:* A frightened animal attacks first to protect itself from a potentially dangerous person. Do not provoke; use a calm, assertive approach with unfriendly people.

- *Be feisty:* Some employees know how to block bullying. Lazy bullies prefer easier targets and avoid assertive people who take appropriate action immediately. Look for your opportunities.

- *Reframe:* Every half empty glass is also half full. Find ways to motivate yourself by saying 'This is a learning experience. The universe wants me to change my life'.

- *Accept reality:* Don't confuse fantasy with reality. All experiences including happy occasions or disaster eventually end, even bullying! Once you accept what is happening, take action to move on; you can make the most of the only life you have.

- *Create your internal stabiliser:* Seafarers find their sea legs to adjust automatically to the rise and fall of waves. Create your own internal stabiliser or coping mechanisms to survive the ups and downs at work, but make sure they suit your current stage — early bullying, intense bullying, injured at home or tackling a new job.

- *Believe that elephants can do more than you think:* Elephants, known for doing heavy labour, can be trained to play football, dance to music, and even paint. You too can learn how to be more assertive by using powerful communication skills.

- *Accept that old dogs do learn new tricks:* Most people, including the elderly, adapt to some electronic technology, such as mobile phones. Obtain feedback from others to identify any of your self-sabotaging behaviours that you can change; for example, looking frustrated, being overly sensitive.

- *Obtain genuine help:* Don't rely on alcohol, drugs, overeating, shopping, gambling, coffee gossip or the smoker's group. Ask for regular support and guidance from those with professional training, responsibility or power to give you the best help within or outside your organisation.

- *Don't bully yourself!* It takes years to survive bullying and heal. Many aspects of your life can be seriously affected so don't be tough on yourself and expect too much too soon!

Reprogram yourself

> Lena's family moved constantly because of her father's army job. It was hard to make friends and she often felt a social failure. She thinks that she's waved the flag for bullies all her life, so didn't tell anyone that she was bullied out of the police force. Now she's becoming assertive and uses skills such as eye contact and speaking clearly. Recent feedback from her bullies shows that they've changed and respect her.[4]

Most computer programs have a short shelf life so you regularly have to update them. Try updating those tired old internal programs that make you powerless and replacing them with empowering ones. Then when you experience a negative thought, stop, identify what is happening and work out what you can do.

Exercise 1

I can do that is a simple mantra. Say it aloud and often to remind yourself that you have the power to confront new challenges, even if they are small ones.

Exercise 2

If you feel powerless or forget to reprogram your negative thoughts into constructive ones, wear a comfortable rubber band around your wrist. If you have a negative thought, pull the rubber band and say *Ouch*. (Don't hurt yourself.) Alternatively say, *I can do that*, and reward yourself with a treat, such as a small piece of dark chocolate.

Exercise 3

Visualise yourself standing outside your workplace describing the bully's behaviours and your organisation's reaction to the waiting media.

One step at a time

> Therese has been off work for 5 years. She is depressed, stressed
> and traumatised. She has neglected housework, gardening and
> grooming, but washes and wears the same clothes every day as
> she has put on weight. She tries to do 10 minutes of housework
> a day and walk more frequently. She is coping on a day-by-day
> basis.

Toddlers gradually learn how to stand and walk. You may feel hopeless
trying to visualise the end to a toxic work environment or fear that you
will never work again. The future is impossible to predict. You might find
the right strategies for managing the bully, and in some companies the
bully might change or leave. You could sell your house and eliminate the
mortgage that padlocked you to that job, or your partner may be trans-
ferred elsewhere. If you are involved with medico–legal compensation or
other forms of legal action, you are in limbo, so resolution can take
months or years. Forget the past and what you should have done, then
focus on what you *can* do now, one step at a time.

Turning points

Although the future can appear bleak and protracted, look for the tiny
turning points that demonstrate that you have changed your attitude and
are behaving like a survivor.

* *Maria began taking a proper lunchbreak and stopped doing extra work.*
* *Robert requested fair shifts and refused to work all the rotten ones.*

- *Tracy felt stronger when she confronted the bully at mediation.*
- *Jane learnt martial arts, which gave her confident body language.*
- *Jocelyn worked every day in her garden to release anger.*
- *Jack undertook study for a new job.*
- *Tom ventilates his anger on an internet self-help group*

How do you assess your progress?

There are many ways of finding out if you're becoming a survivor. Here are some examples.

- You look the bully straight in the eye.
- You confront or block the bully.
- The bully respects you more, or is more careful around you.
- Management is actively supporting you.
- Colleagues are more supportive and friendlier.
- Your sleep patterns are normal.
- You are feeling and looking happier.
- You receive positive feedback from family, friends or workmates.
- You identify positive turning points.
- You are planning to leave that job.

Look after yourself

> **❝**At a workplace bullying support group, I learned a little about
> how different people cope with the trauma of workplace
> bullying. Linda loves her garden and sailing, Sarah enjoys
> sewing, Jo plays soccer to release anger, Dina collects news-
> paper articles about bullying, Lena bakes cupcakes, Anna
> makes hats and Rena makes dips and cookies.
>
> Some time ago the group went to the seaside for several days.
> They described the experience as extremely beneficial; a switch-
> ing-off from their stresses. At times it was intense and over-
> whelming, but they also had time for sharing and caring, fun
> and tears and time to be alone. They felt safe being with others
> who understood. I marvelled at the pleasure on their faces
> when they shared a swim and spa, and when they laughed (for
> the first time) about a day off from bullying. **❞**

Dealing with workplace bullying can be toxic whether you are a target,
bully, witness, manager, lawyer, researcher, investigator or mental health
professional. Brave pioneers, such as the journalist Andrea Adams, who
wrote *Bullying at Work: How to Confront and Overcome It*[1] in 1992 and
Tim Field, who founded the UK National Workplace Bullying Advice
Line in the same year, died young while pursuing justice for victims. Be
warned! Don't allow the toxic impact from bullies, workmates or dysfunctional workplaces to jam your emotional system and endanger your wellbeing. Whether you are being bullied at work or dealing with the fallout
since leaving, you need all the emotional and physical energy you can
gather until your whole life is back on track.

Take responsibility for your wellbeing

> 'I had a complex medical injury that was so bad that at one stage
> I couldn't fill out any forms. So I created my support team,
> including my doctor, psychiatrist, psychologist and masseur.'

Treating some physical injuries such as a broken bone is generally straight-forward, whereas treating cancer is far more complicated and varies from patient to patient depending on a range of health and medical factors. Your workplace bullying injury is likewise complex and its treatment will need to be very personalised. However the diagnosis and treatment of work-created conditions such as chronic anxiety, depression and work-place bullying trauma are under-researched and the health professions do not as yet have access to clear data on why and how bad workplace bullying can be. You will need to be strong in taking overall responsibility for your wellbeing during your recovery and encourage those around you to take an individual approach, based upon your specific needs. This will involve a variety of therapeutic approaches.

Commonsense therapy

Sleep

You need a good night's sleep. Your bedroom should be designed for sleeping — it's not an office or a worry workspace. Try the tips below:

- Write down any painful issues and leave the list in another room.
- Practise a calming routine before going to sleep; for example, a bubble bath, soft music, incense or perfumed room spray.
- Use suitable herbs — chamomile and valerian tonic aids sleep; sprinkle a few drops of calming lavender oil onto your pillow.
- If you wake in the middle of the night get up and have some diversion-ary tasks prepared: read a magazine, listen to music, or do something tedious such as ironing.

Food

Check that your diet is providing you with the optimum strength, vitality and comfort to cope. If necessary, arrange to have healthy meals delivered if you don't feel like cooking.

- Eat vitamin-rich foods to give you more energy and less anxiety, such as fish, lean meat, grains, honey, fresh fruit and vegetables.
- Eat less processed foods, fatty meat, and foods high in saturated fats.
- Reduce the sugar content in your food to lower the glycemic index; as an example, a sweet potato is healthier than an ordinary potato.

- Eat three regular meals per day to keep your metabolism efficient.
- Drink at least six glasses of water a day to cleanse your internal system.
- Try and avoid coffee, tea and carbonated drinks that contain the stimulant caffeine as these can exacerbate feelings of stress. Try herbal teas instead.
- Take vitamin and mineral supplements to compensate for any dietary deficiencies you may not be aware of. This can reduce symptoms, rebuild and maintain your immune system and provide extra energy. Examples include multivitamins, omega-3 oils (from wild salmon) and vitamin D to reduce depression.
- A few pieces of dark chocolate (70–85% cocoa has a lower fat content than normal chocolate) can help when we feel stressed. Cocoa has been used for thousands of years for tribal rituals and healing. Dark chocolate can help you feel calmer, relieving stress and depression by releasing feel-good hormones such as serotonin and endorphins. But make sure that you don't binge as then you will feel worse!

Physical exercise

Exercise provides a wide range of health benefits. It helps you breathe in more life-giving oxygen, counteracts negative emotions by activating feel-good hormones, and assists in your circulatory and digestive health as well as helping with bone density. Regular exercise will help you reduce your level of anger, anxiety and depression.

- Find a simple, regular exercise regime appropriate to your age and physical capabilities. A good gym or personal trainer with experience in rehabilitative exercise and injury treatment is a good place to start.
- Build your level of physical fitness to give you more energy to cope and confront stressors. Try walking, push-ups, cycling, dancing or the gym.
- Aim for at least 4 hours a week or 20 minutes of exercise a day, breaking it into smaller portions if necessary, such as 10 minutes twice day.

Make your home life more comfortable

> *Matt is a builder and loves surfing. 'Surf's up!' He goes off with his mates while clients wait, and he works when waves are flat.*

It is extremely unhealthy to obsess about bullying 24 hours a day. You need time for your recovery, such as an occasional mental health day, or you might obtain medical permission to use your sick leave. If you are too injured to work, find activities that distract you and provide a temporary break from your stressful existence.

- Make sure your home is a safe, supportive, relaxing environment in which to recharge your energies and forget work.
- If your emotional stresses are impacting on your family and home life, obtain professional help before the reactions of those around you begin to impact back on yourself.
- Find a special place or sanctuary to hide at times when you just need to be by yourself, such as your bedroom, a garden, or even a local coffee shop.
- Rearrange household chores so that others help you.
- Obtain more hugs from family and friends and even soft toys.
- Invest in a pet — nature's empathy providers and wonderful healers! Pet therapy reduces stress, improves physical health and emotional wellbeing.
- Slow down your pace of life a little — stop to smell the flowers, cook slow food, potter among plants, read in bed, enjoy a bath, learn a new hobby.
- Take some 'R & R' — find time for a real break away, or have some quality time socialising or pursuing outdoor activities.
- Remember to maintain friendships — share a brief update and then an activity, try movies, camping, exercise.

Make your workplace more comfortable

While you can't restructure your workplace you can try to lighten the stress levels by actively focusing on nonwork-related aspects during your breaks. No matter what your employer might say, a worker's break is their personal time and there is no need to remain switched on and in work mode if it is lunchtime. Pursue some appropriate activities that you enjoy.

- Play with puzzles on your mobile phone, read a book, or venture into cyberspace (making sure if using work computers that you remain within your organisation's rules about their use).

- Try and make your work area as calming and as comforting as possible by bringing in personal objects such as photos or ornaments.

- Practise some attention training — focusing upon the sounds, sights, scents, colours and textures around you.

- Eat your lunch away from work, in a park, or go for a walk.

Spiritual health

Trees need strong roots to cope with wind. Many informal studies show that people with a strong belief system cope better with stress. The belief seems to strengthen and sustain a person's survival mechanisms. This means finding purpose and meaning in your life, and knowing what comforts and motivates you, is an important part of your self-care. Caring for those around you and receiving the support of family and friends who love you are important in this process. So too is enjoying other parts of your life that bring you deep and calming feelings of wellness and a belief in yourself and your part in the world. You don't need to belong to an organised religion to practise such spiritual health, though it may help to talk regularly to your minister, rabbi, priest, or imam. You can meditate or pray at any place of prayer in which you feel comfortable, or alternatively, practise your own rituals such as lighting candles, reciting psalms, or listening to religious music.

Medical health

> Mary found that her medication placed less strain on her family and friends and made her driving safer. Her doctor was very supportive and even phoned her employer and told him that if she was bullied again, he'd give her another certificate to stay off work longer. When her employer realised what Mary's health effects from the bullying were costing him in lost work and increased payrolls, the bullying actually stopped!

If you are being bullied, you need the regular support of a general practitioner with whom you can share a constructive, caring, long-term working relationship. If your doctor does not understand the nature of workplace bullying — the individual and/or systemic causes and the difference between stress, anxiety disorders and trauma — you should try to make them aware by providing more information, such as this book or any recent articles you have collected. Be wary of general practitioners who are not interested in workplace bullying, have a blind spot about its toxic impact, or have limited skills for dealing with trauma. They may in fact blame you for your injuries. They cannot offer any long-term support and may prescribe drugs inappropriate to your psychological state. Alternatively, find a doctor who specialises in occupational health and is prepared to consult and collaborate with your personal doctor. An effective doctor will:

- document your emotional pain and any related physical and psychological symptoms, such as increase in blood pressure, sleep problems, or weight gain

- record the timeframe of any reported injuries and major traumatic incidents

- assist with medico–legal claims once you have provided them with all the relevant information

- provide official reports explaining causes and descriptions of your injury

- refer you to other health professionals, such as psychologists and/or psychiatrists, and collaborate with them

- advise you on ways to maintain physical health to help with your stress

- prescribe medication to alleviate symptoms of anxiety, anger, depression, trauma, or panic attack

- discuss any concerns about your medication

- help to influence employers and insurance agencies to treat workplace bullying victims with respect by communicating with them in a professional and caring manner.

A warning about medical care

Medication may be useful with painful or severe symptoms of anxiety, depression and trauma[2] although sometimes it can be inappropriate, ineffective or harmful. It cannot replace the counselling you require to deal with your painful experiences or develop future bully blocking skills. You may require both at various stages.[3] Be aware too that sometimes a placebo works as well as medication,[4] so always remember that when agreeing to medication you should follow it as instructed and accept that it will work. Don't swallow a pill and blame yourself for having to seek medical help. Remind yourself regularly that your injury was caused by many factors, the major one being your negligent workplace, and that your medical treatment is helping you recover.

Alternative health therapies

> 'When I have a bad memory I use my "flashback replacement therapy" to visualise a photo of a pretty flower rather than the trauma.'

There are many traditional or natural therapies you can investigate to help rebuild your physical and emotional health. Alternative treatments need to be safe, however. Just because something is labelled 'natural' doesn't mean it can't be harmful. The Romans were fond of using belladonna, or the deadly nightshade plant, to poison rivals. Alternative therapies and treatments should not be capable of causing side effects with medications (e.g., St John's Wort, which is incompatible with a range of prescribed medication). Always ask your doctor first. Therapies to consider include:

- those from natural health practitioners, such as naturopaths, homoeopaths, aromatherapists
- mind–body treatments, such as massage, relaxation, meditation, yoga, Chinese medicine, Ayurvedic medicine, reiki, tai chi, Feldenkrais, Qigong, or martial arts
- aromatherapy — essential plant oils reduce stress, encourage relaxation, foster concentration, release emotional pain and promote well-being. They are used through inhalation or massage.
- herbal remedies that strengthen your immune system, relieve anxiety and reduce depression, such as Bach Rescue Remedy.

Psychological therapy

> 'The cognitive–behaviour therapy (CBT) really helped me. It put things into perspective, so if I'm up against brick walls I cope better. I write down negative outcomes and turn them into positive ones. I consider the bully's perspective and their support team; that helps find a potential way though the dilemma. Therapy keeps me away from the door of the pit. I know when to

step back, relax and then return to battle. Therapy helps you recognise warning signs and act on them before too much damage sets in, and keeps bitterness at bay.'

'My therapist stops me drifting into nowhere and losing myself. She anchors me to life and tries to motivate me to cope and move on.'

Many people believe there is a stigma attached to consulting a mental health professional. However, the trauma produced by workplace bullying can cause a complex injury that requires treatment and long-term support by a psychologist and/or psychiatrist. They can help you manoeuvre your way around the minefield of abusive work practices and assist you to think objectively about your options. Their wisdom and skills help you deal with your emotional pain, thereby neutralising the toxic psychological effects your body can create from its own hormones. Without good psychological therapy you are at risk of further injuring your physical and mental health, leaving you seriously stressed, depressed or traumatised for years.

Even though the current evidence base for the effective treatment of victims of workplace bullying is still young, your therapist should be able to work effectively with you. As they and their colleagues become more aware of the extent and damage of workplace bullying, it is hoped that more formalised training and research will contribute greatly to the field.

Some victims will, however, feel that the bully has the problem and is the one who needs psychological therapy, not themselves. Although it may be true that the bully can also benefit from therapy, unfortunately you are the one injured and suffering debilitating effects in work and home life. The bully may have the power to continue, and you need to use effective skills to manage and block them. If you cannot contemplate consulting a psychologist or psychiatrist, find a professional life coach who is also a registered psychologist. Their life-improvement approach may be more easy for you to accept than a traditional treatment model. However, effective psychological treatment will involve an acceptance of where you are now and a positive goal for the future, no matter how it is presented.

Choosing your therapist

Whether you are shopping for reliable shoes, a car or a therapist, you need to do your homework well to ensure you find what is suitable. You might start by consulting your general practitioner, lawyer, bullying support groups, the internet or professional associations. Your therapist needs to be

CHAPTER EIGHT | Look after yourself

ethical, empathic and trustworthy. They need clear professional boundaries to provide you with unbiased, objective support to empower you, without being unduly influenced by their own belief systems or personal bullying experiences. Depending on the type and severity of your workplace bullying trauma you may require more than one therapist, such as a psychiatrist to provide medication, and a psychologist to provide counselling, assertiveness skills training, relaxation skills, anger management, marital counselling, parenting skills and vocational guidance. If you find at any time that the counselling process is harmful, not confidential, or nontherapeutic, then discuss the situation with your therapist. If it cannot be improved, then shop around for someone else more suitable. An effective therapist will:

- enable you to feel safe and comfortable and share any distress or concerns — including during treatment, which could be psychologically painful at times

- understand the biochemical, psychological and social impact of workplace trauma and have experience in assisting victims or be prepared to learn about it

- have a flexible attitude and a variety of therapies to suit your needs

- be able to distinguish between bullying targets who require coping strategies and bullying victims who have been severely traumatised

- understand when you forget an appointment or cancel because you cannot cope that day, and not pressure you to come regularly

- be available if necessary for years, and accessible out of hours for desperate occasions

- preferably not be connected to your organisation or torn between loyalty to whoever pays them and their ethical responsibilities to you.

Cost of treatment

Psychological and psychiatric treatment can be expensive although both private and government medical benefits schemes now cover mental health treatments more comprehensively than in the past. In Australia, Medicare subsidies are available for certain designated psychological therapy by an approved provider. Some state governments provide for employee treatment under workers compensation schemes although the extent of coverage

BULLY BLOCKING AT WORK: A Self-Help Guide for Employees and Managers **113** varies. If possible, try to get your organisation to fund your treatment. Unfortunately, you may need more than the few sessions provided through most employer assistance schemes. Perhaps you can extend these sessions by negotiating with your employer or the therapist.

Therapy

> Melanie learnt how to deal with her bully boss in five sessions. Once she labelled him as a saltwater crocodile, she changed her attitude and behaviours. He stopped.

You can learn how to block most bullies in about four to eight sessions provided you seek help early from an experienced therapist and before you are so psychologically injured that you are unable to carry out appropriate bully blocking strategies. If you need time off from work to cope or you have been forced out of your job, then you have probably been injured. In this case, while you may not realise it, the healing process will take longer (maybe years), especially if exacerbated by an ongoing medico–legal mine-field. You require consistent, compassionate, unconditional support and counselling. You cannot deal with it alone, nor should family and friends shoulder all your burdens as they too will suffer unfairly.

Your therapist will help you deal with your injuries and provide techniques for coping with anxiety, anger, depression and trauma. During your therapy sessions you will discover more about yourself and find strengths and vulnerabilities you did not know you possessed. You can use these insights to energise your hidden potential. Then you can heal, rebuild your personal and professional life and move on.

According to the US psychologist Ronnie Janoff-Bulman, trauma victims need to work through their toxic experiences by talking about their trauma-related thoughts and feelings.[5] Although you may have shared segments of the bullying game with others, when you share your story for the first time in therapy, it reflects a raw, unpractised quality, in contrast to the rehearsed presentation of a professional speaker. The story seems to tumble out like pieces from a jumbled jigsaw puzzle. However, you will eventually create a special flow to your story, which will desensitise and release your pain, validate your experiences and provide a more comprehensive perspective. Unlike most other victims of trauma, you may need to release as many details of your story as you can and revisit them hundreds of times, obsessing over details for years. Creating your story is a necessary part of your healing process.

Therapeutic goals

Your therapist will help you set goals to work through in your sessions. They might include some of the following:

- Identifying painful symptoms and releasing traumatic feelings such as stress, fear, anger, shame, humiliation, frustration, guilt.
- Reframing your story to understand why you were targeted and injured.
- Reducing your psychological paralysis by exploring the emotional impact of the bullying.
- Relearning how to move freely between your thoughts, feelings and memories about the past, present and future.
- Distinguishing between behaviours that stem from normal functioning and those produced by trauma.
- Obtaining the validation to heal.
- Attaining assertive social survival skills to effectively block bullies.
- Achieving effective personal and family relationships that have been damaged by the stress of your injuries.
- Being able to comfortable deal with previously stressful questions, such as *Why aren't you at work?* (e.g., *I've been injured by workplace bullying,* or *I'm currently taking legal action.*)
- Empowering you to take control of your life and reconstructing your personality to find safer directions to allow a return to your former workplace or find new career directions.
- The healthy completion of the mourning for your losses and the strength to move on.

Types of therapy

There are many different types of psychological therapy and while research has shown that there are no perfect 100% success rate treatments for psychological difficulties (much the same as for most medical treatments), therapies that are matched well to personality types, cognitive styles and the types of mental problems presented are more effective. Be wary of any therapies that may be in vogue but don't address your immediate or long term needs. Despite this, the ultimate success of any therapeutic model depends on the quality of the relationship between you and your therapist.

The effective basis to a lengthy therapeutic relationship is a supportive and restorative approach which provides validation, regular support in dealing with trauma, assistance in the pursuit of justice where appropriate and the rebuilding of social and emotional resilience. Therapies known to provide useful techniques for stress, depression and trauma include: Rogerian therapy, Ericksonian therapy, psychotherapy, family systems therapy, narrative therapy, eye movement desensitisation reprogramming (EMDR), cognitive–behaviour therapy (CBT), traumatic incident reduction (TIR), rational emotive therapy (RET), neurolinguistic programming (NLP), mindfulness, psychodrama and Gestalt therapy.

Workplace bullying support groups

'This group gave me privacy — it's easier to talk with strangers, there's no risk. I could express myself openly. I saw the typical bullying pattern emerge. I was betrayed by my CEO, colleagues, union, insurance company and lawyers. I realised that it wasn't my fault, many intelligent, competent employees are singled out by bullies. I received empathy — everyone knows how I feel and I know how they feel. I don't need to depend on friends and family who care but don't understand. We laugh together through our tears. If the group had existed previously, I would have made fewer mistakes. They share information on where to get help and support you through court cases.'

In Europe there are now clinics specifically designed to treat victims of workplace bullying. In Australia this does not happen. But support groups for victims of bullying are beginning to catch on. In 2002 one of my own clients was feeling extremely isolated and wanted to meet other victims. That's when I decided to start a support group, and the groups are still running and proving highly effective. Sometimes one person turns up, other times there are many. It runs for over 3 hours monthly, with lots of sharing, the occasional speaker or outing, return-to-work issues, afternoon tea, and a touch of pet therapy from my two pampered papillon dogs.

A group experience is totally different to seeing a therapist on your own. You tend to express your story differently to the group, providing another form of healing. It is therapeutic and validating to share your story with others who understand, and you experience relief to know that you are not that different and share so much in common. You will find that other targets and victims are just as competent at their work as you were, unlike the

picture your bully boss may have painted. You will develop more confidence to speak to others about bullying and take action.

Members of workplace bullying support groups help each other at court, write letters together, share their knowledge and experiences, discuss their options and socialise informally — meeting for coffee and exercise. The group stops you focusing solely on your own problems and reminds you to care for others. In fact, many bully targets lose a part of their social life when they leave a workplace, so the support group can rebuild social confidence and provide you with unique social support. As you recover and move on, you can rebuild a new social group with common interests beyond bullying.

If you do not have access to a support group either locally or from within your profession or union, you could encourage your therapist to run one. A therapist can provide objectivity, skilled facilitation of group discussion, and the secretarial support to ensure longevity. Sometimes insurance companies will pay for any costs associated with support groups. If you cannot find a group, you might like to start your own with your work colleagues, outside work hours, provided there are no repercussions. I know of a successful group begun by a woman in my state who found a free local hall, free media to advertise it and assistance to coordinate it. The internet now also provides a way for groups to come together without travelling beyond their own house. In any group it is important to follow set ground rules (see box below) and remember when sharing to include the past (or yesterday), the present (or today) and the future (or tomorrow). If you find the idea of a support group just focusing on bullying a bit too stressful, you could consider a group that does other things as well, such as holding hobby meetings, bringing a plate for lunch, going on group walks, or similar activities.

Workplace bullying support group rules

- *Respect confidentiality.*
- *Give everyone a fair go.*
- *No-one is allowed bully anyone else.*
- *Care for others.*
- *Everyone brings refreshments.*

Bully blocking at work

❝*I've been wearing really nice business suits to work and using body language to appear confident. I'm interacting with people at all levels from top to bottom. No more glaring looks from the 'stupidvisor' today. I looked her right in the eye the whole time when she was looking at me during our daily meeting. I was silent most of the time, except when I needed to share information. I brought a notepad and took notes on the work assignments. When she hit on a particularly nasty point, I told her that I wanted to clarify her statement. I repeated it back to her, asking if I understood that correctly and then calmly wrote it down, showing no emotion.*❞

Bullying involves the abuse of power. Although as a target of bullying you have less power, you need to take action to protect yourself. Even the act of trying to redress the power imbalance, no matter what the actual outcome is, will kickstart your survival instinct. The bonus of early activation is that you are less likely to suffer the harmful effects of too many stress hormones still being released by your body's flight or fight response, long after the bullying has ceased. Dealing with bullying in the workplace early and effectively is vital to ensure you become a survivor of bullying, not a victim.

There are three basic ways to deal with bullying:

- Passively, where you retreat, complain, and do nothing.
- Aggressively, where you fight back, retaliate, and/or become defensive.
- Assertively, by blocking or managing the bullying.

Reacting passively or aggressively in the face of a bully, as in all conflict situations, is least likely to achieve a fair and balanced outcome. Bully blocking on the other hand can facilitate a better resolution. If you question, research, and assertively confront with constructive action (when safe to do so), you empower yourself. The bully blocking process involves assessing the situation, maintaining records, doing research and investigating your legal rights and support structures. It means understanding your work culture, balancing your skills at diplomacy and assertiveness (possibly becoming feisty), and working the system to look after yourself. Eventually these actions should block the bullying, help you survive, and allow you to move on. Even if you can't achieve a full resolution to the bullying, your conscience will know that you have done the best that you can. Meanwhile you can place the ethical and legal responsibility for stopping bullying onto the managers at work who condoned the bullying.

Assessing your bully

Earlier in this book I described the main types of bullies: the saltwater crocodiles or serial bully who take you into the death roll, such as the manager who boasted that he 'operates by fear and surprise', and the fowls who play foul with the attitude that 'everyone does it' and bully from habit or circumstance.

Serial bullies have a long history of bullying because they have developed excellent skills to justify their behaviours. Their games disguise their total lack of empathy and responsibility for their behaviours. You can't be assertive with crocodiles; you need to anticipate and block their cunning games. However, the fowls who play foul can be empathic to your situation, as long as you don't threaten them. They may respond positively to a constructive assertive communication by you or your manager.

Bullies can be extremely subtle and will retaliate against any effort to confront them. They can become very devious, manipulating others to bully you, or intensifying the bullying. Thus you need to assess the type of bully you are dealing with and their reasons for bullying you. Does the bully care about your feelings or not? Perhaps they don't realise how hurtful they are. Maybe they are part of a bullying chain and pass the bullying behaviours along. Are you their only target or are there others? Look behind the scene. Are they hiding an affair, plotting to get your job for a friend or angry that you did or didn't get their job? If you were walking in their shoes, what would you be feeling, thinking and doing? Asking these questions can also help decide if you are being unreasonable, behaving inappropriately, or unconsciously attracting bullying behaviours.

Use the bully's regular pattern of behaviour to predict what they might do when they are confronted and work out how to protect yourself. For

Remember:

- *Nobody likes being called a bully.*
- *Bully bashing is retaliation.*
- *Blame equals inflame.*
- *Focus on a bully's behaviours, not their personality.*
- *Bullies deny and fight back.*
- *Bullying is difficult to prove without witnesses, records or specific injuries.*

example, perhaps the bullying is worse on Mondays, or after a meeting with the boss. Always remember, when deciding on appropriate tactics to deal with your bully, not to start bullying someone yourself.

If you have been accused of using bullying behaviours, don't become defensive or offensive. You have more to gain personally, professionally and financially by dealing with your stresses and frustration effectively, than abusing your power. Beware that any show of disrespect may boomerang back onto you! Just imagine that video cameras are monitoring every employee. Would you be proud of what the video shows about your behaviours? Obtain constructive feedback from a variety of sources. If true, apologise, express empathy and learn more effective relating skills. If false, show your evidence.

Auditing your employer or organisation

Have you ever been to an expensive restaurant and visited the bathroom? It's wonderful when the bathroom looks as luxurious as the dining room, though deeply disappointing when the elegant facade hides shabby facilities. A similar distortion, deceit or inconsistency may apply to your workplace today even though it was not evident when you began work. Originally the culture may have mirrored your beliefs and values, but an organisational change, such as a new manager or new policies, may have altered the landscape. Perhaps you focused on your job while being oblivious to the poisonous politics polluting your workplace.

If there are explicit antibullying policies at your workplace, then look for the gap between what is supposed to happen and what actually does happen. Check out whether the organisation really values and cares for you, or whether it is just a token attempt. Determine how your expectations of support, equity and justice will be met. The fact is that while ethical and empathic work cultures can be socially responsible, toxic cultures are not. Whatever the case, you can't accept things as they first appear. You need to investigate, challenge and ask questions. You need to find managers who listen and take action, or go as high as possible to obtain help when necessary.

Establishing a paper trail and maintaining accurate records

> Kate worked in a plant nursery. Her boss wanted her to leave so he placed her in a dark office, without windows, covered in graffiti. The roof fell on her one day and water ran down the wall. She was ordered to work alone; staff were forbidden to speak to her. Eventually, she met with the insurance officers and her boss. When she showed them the photos of her office, a thick folder of notes, and mentioned possible media interest, he paid her out!

It is vital that you record everything that has happened. Some bullying incidents are insidious and, when taken singly, appear trivial and harmless. However, a comprehensive, objective record of incidents, including dates and descriptions, provides a degree of credibility not possible with a single incident. These records will reveal a cumulative pattern of events. Without them, people may believe the bully. Records are very important for your union, lawyer, therapist and doctor, and may also persuade your employer against going to court. If you take legal action, your written record may increase your employer's liability for failing to respect their duty of care to you.

Make sure that you inform everyone, including senior managers, about the bullying and any subsequent actions, via written memos, face-to-face interviews, voice-recordings or email, and ensure you keep copies of all material at home. These records will demonstrate how the bully acts in the workplace and retaliates against any attempts to stop him. To help focus your thoughts on what information to include, look at the Bully Record Sheet shown on pages 127–128 of this chapter.

You should question, clarify and record everything that is discussed and resolved throughout the progress of a bullying complaint at work,

Workplace bullying audit

- *Establish whether the bully's demands and behaviours are reasonable for your job description or not; for example, talk to others in the organisation, such as the previous position holder or others doing the same work, look at the job description or employment contract.*

- *Does your employer, manager or human resources staff truly regard workplace bullying as a serious hazard or just pretend it is?*

- *Are colleagues encouraged to support and protect you; to join the bully gang; or are they petrified too?*

- *Is management ignorant or just terrified of vicarious liability?*

- *Does your employer believe in adversarial tactics, or do they collaborate respectfully to resolve differences?*

- *Does your employer blame individuals — the target or bully — or do they acknowledge that bullying is maintained by systemic dysfunction?*

- *Does your organisation employ effective independent investigations and internal dispute resolution procedures for dealing with bullying?*

- *Does your organisation implement appropriate sanctions for bullying behaviours?*

- *Is the bullying camouflaging mismanagement, fraud or unethical behaviours?*

- *Does your organisation acknowledge your perception of feeling bullied and unsafe, independent of any investigation into the facts?*

- *Does your organisation demonstrate its immediate commitment to creating a safe, equitable solution?*

- *Does your organisation use any tactics to delay, handicap or try to eliminate the problem; for example, refer you for a psychiatric assessment, but not the bully?*

- *Does the organisation check what outcome you hope to achieve when you report the bullying?*

- *Does the organisation initiate massive investigations when a simple chat would suffice?*

including treatment and return-to-work meetings. Confirm all discussions or meetings by email to record your evidence, time and date to avoid anyone pleading ignorance about what took place. If you don't receive replies when you know the person has received them, email and label their lack of reply as an acceptance. This will force them to write back to you if they wish to dispute your initial communication.

For serious cases of bullying, you might like to obtain legal advice about designing your letters or emails to ensure your paper trail is useful to any legal counsel in future confrontations. Remember too, before signing any confidential agreements that may be presented to you, to find out how they will impact on what you can say afterwards.

When requesting any information for your records from your manager, human resources staff, a therapist or lawyer, make sure you check their verbal and nonverbal feedback when you are asking them. Then assess who you can trust, who can help and who will do nothing or possibly even sabotage you.

What to do at home

- Store all records securely at home, away from your employer and bully.

- Use your home computer and/or a loose-leaf folder.

- Divide your folder into sections; for example, bullying incidents, medical and employer notes.

- Inform your doctor, therapist and lawyer, who must maintain their records.

- Record every incident with a timeline of events including the date, location and time it occurred.

- Describe each bullying-related incident simply and concisely; for example, 'He yelled at me in a closed office for four hours', 'I told him that micromanagement is unfair', 'I was left out of the email information loop on five occasions'.

- Record words spoken by your bully/manager in bold and colour; for example, 'YOU IDIOT!'

- Record every occasion where you took the recommended steps to stop the bullying and reported it, verbally or preferably in writing (email is best), to a supervisor, manager, human resources staff.

- Record exactly what the company did and when they failed to intervene and protect you from further bullying.

- Record if management exacerbated the bullying (noting the actual times and dates), such as when you told a manager and they retaliated with a performance review.

- Keep all evidence, such as nasty text messages, emails, photos, torn clothing, voice-recordings, telephone bugs (with legal advice), phone records, handwritten notes.

- Record how the bullying has injured you, physically, emotionally, economically, socially and so on; for example: 'I felt … when X did …'.

- If you have been forced to leave work, describe how this has affected you.

- Record all your associated financial costs and losses for any compensation claim, including visits and fares (mileage) to your doctor or psychologist, associated physical therapies, lost wages, and medications.

- Collect copies of all performance appraisals, promotions, letters, cards or memos that indicate your high standard of work and relationship skills. This list includes managers, other employees, clients, customers, patients and students. Where possible, try and obtain references and written feedback for future use. You may need this written material as proof of your prebullying level of competence and to counteract any accusations from bully and employer alike.

- Note down the details of all phone calls, letters, documents and visits to lawyers, doctors, psychiatrists, psychologists and the like.

- Obtain written statements and affidavits as soon as possible from other targets or witnesses. Obtain their private contact details if you need further contact. They may move away later or be pressured to renege and betray.

- Record other stressful or difficult work conditions, such as inadequate computer systems, the boss's affair with a secretary, staff redundancies, a lack of staff meetings.

- Record your bully's work performance and evidence of their mismanagement, retaliation, fraud, malpractice, misuse of government funding, abuse of company policies or legal requirements. This evidence may be used as leverage with senior management, assist police or your lawyer and validate a complaint to the bully's professional association. Make sure your evidence is objective and nonvindictive.

- Record the impact of the bullying on witnesses and the company; for example, unhappy clients, expensive mistakes, high turnover of witnesses.

- Include any research into workplace bullying that is relevant; for example, bullying in the nursing profession, or symptoms of posttraumatic stress disorder.

A personal record

When surviving at work seems like wading through quicksand, or when you are forced to stay home with an injury, the days can merge into one another. A personal record — your yesterday, today and tomorrow — can help you feel less paralysed and begin empowering you to move forward. It is important to consider your past or yesterday, the present or today, and the future or tomorrow. You can use a notebook or computer to record your activities, feelings or events. The record may include medical visits, gardening days, good moments, bad memories, visiting friends and important mail. By

Bully record sheet

Dates bullying behaviours occurred:

Name(s) of bully:

Behaviours: For example, shouting, interrupting, threatening, excluding, spreading malicious rumours or cyber lies.

Frequency: For example, daily, weekly, monthly, occasionally.

Locations: For example, lunchroom, open office, closed office, boardroom, home phone/computer. Draw a map if required.

My reactions: For example, 'I try to defend myself', 'I am too scared so I say nothing'.

Witnesses and their reactions: Who intervened and helped? Who did nothing? Who made it worse? Who else is being bullied?

Who you reported it to at work: For example, the line manager, HR, occupational health and safety union, lawyer.

When you reported it:

How you reported it: For example, verbally, email, or by note.

What assistance were you given: For example, investigation, employee counselling, mediation, or transfer.
- *These people were helpful …*
- *These people were unsympathetic …*
- *These people tried but weren't successful …*
- *These people made it worse and bullied me too …*

Actions your organisation took: For example, did they validate your experience? Do you feel safe now? Did they do nothing? Did they make it worse?

Others you have told outside work: For example, your partner, friends, or a doctor.

How these others have been helpful: For example, medication, counselling, sharing housework.

People who have been unhelpful:

'I believe that the bully …'
- *Is fooling around and doesn't mean to upset me: Yes/No*
- *Is still a nice person: Yes/No*
- *Was my friend: Yes/No*
- *Became a bully after a disagreement: Yes/No*

(continued over)

Bully record sheet *(continued)*

- *Enjoys hurting me: Yes/No*
- *Follows their bully boss: Yes/No*
- *Bullies other staff: Yes/No*

Other things happening within your organisation: *For example, profits are down, a takeover is imminent, a new manager needs to prove himself, a culture of bullying seems to be normal, or company antibullying policies are not enforced or monitored.*

---

writing down what is happening in your life, you are more likely to validate your day-to-day experiences and may even feel better.

What to do at work

Do not leave anything relevant about the workplace bullying in your work phone, computer or filing cabinet. However, you should record your physical or psychological injures in a work-accident book if one exists at your organisation. Even if your manager objects to this you should still try, as well recording any bullying incidents you witnessed happening to others.

You can take notes or openly voice-record the bully while they are bullying you. If you are confronted, tell the bully that you cannot remember anything when you are stressed and so you need to record the conversation so you will be clear about what is being discussed. If you want to record any conversation without the other party knowing, you must consult a lawyer first. Make sure that you save all relevant work files on a removable drive instead of emailing it home.

Some examples of the types of questions to ask your bully:

- Confirmation: 'You did say that I have to check with you each time I leave the office?'
- Clarify: 'Exactly what do you mean that I've a personality problem?'
- Proof: 'What's your written evidence about my poor attitude?'
- Review: 'Did you just stand over me and shout in my face?'
- Challenge: 'Why do you need to check my emails *when you aren't checking other people's?*'

Beware the organisational bully backlash

Conflict can occur anywhere. If everyone involved in a conflict has the opportunity to discuss their concerns and resolve them, as parents do with children, the dispute ends and the damage is resolved. Everyone moves on. Unfortunately, when you are engaged in the process of bully blocking you may find that your organisation treats criticism, complaint or confrontation as a break in the level of 'trust' you share as an employee. If your employer lacks appropriate collaborative mechanisms for resolving conflict or the dispute resolution processes are contaminated, then you need to be aware of some of the consequences of making your complaint. The procedure may attack the prevailing culture, and threaten bullies and adversarial managers. To try and mitigate the effects of this you must fulfil your basic work requirements and avoid any work performance issues while you are engaging in the complaints process. Aim to be polite, respectful and proceed cautiously while pursuing your concerns. Consider the risks and repercussions that follow any complaint and obtain support to cope with any backlash.

The sorts of events that can occur in a bully backlash include:

- you being labelled as a 'personality problem', a 'troublemaker', 'difficult', or 'not a team player'.

- management executing a backflip and blaming you for bullying them, or using performance or discipline reviews against you, despite evidence of your earlier good work history.

- claims that you are difficult to work with, followed by isolation or a transfer to another department and even redundancy.

- your manager may refuse to give you a reference, and spread gossip that prevents you from obtaining alternative employment in your industry.

What do you really want to achieve with your bully blocking?

'This bully tortured me for 5 years, he did it before me, and is still doing it to other employees but he no longer bothers me. I kept a journal for 5 years after he launched a full-frontal attack on me at staff meetings. I put my objections about him in writing to our attorneys and the city had to pay big bucks for a high-powered investigation. They asked me what I wanted. I said, "Not money. What I want is to not see him. I don't want to

report to him for my work. I want nothing to do with him." I got that wish and I am the envy of everyone who still has to deal with his bullying behaviour.'

Mary's bully was forced to give a verbal apology in a criminal court. Yet the bully's 'sorry' was burped out with a venomous twist of her shoulder, like a rude teenager. The written apology delivered later was couched in superficial lawyer's language designed to satisfy a legal requirement and nothing else. Mary never received a genuine one.

All targets need validation and a safe workplace. They usually prefer reconciliation and restoration, not retribution or pitiful compensation payouts. Unless your organisation uses a restorative model, most dispute intervention processes cause bullies to feel sorry for the trouble the bullying has caused themselves rather than its impact on you the target. Therefore your likelihood of a genuine apology is poor. It is important to identify at the start of the bully blocking exactly what you want to achieve out of this process apart from getting the bullying to stop. This will depend on what you have experienced and the organisation's reactions. It may be one or a number of the ideas listed here:

- validation or acknowledgment
- an apology (genuine or pseudo)
- a safe workplace for all
- a fair resolution
- revenge or payback
- financial compensation
- improved company practices
- another position or retraining away from the bully
- the demotion or removal of the bully
- professional restitution
- reinstatement of leave that you have taken as a result of the bullying.

Bully blocking tips

> *'Running the gauntlet' comes from an old Swedish military pun-ishment to send the victim through a double line of men, each armed with a club to beat him as he passed. When someone runs the gauntlet they're exposed to risk at every step.*

Dealing with bullying is a huge challenge. Most companies don't have a magic solution, and you will be the one initiating the process of con-fronting the bullying and finding ways to resolve its toxic impact. You will need to consider many options, risks and repercussions as you proceed. It's like running a gauntlet. But your best chance of making it through and out the other end as a survivor is to use the bully blocking process. Whenever your safety is threatened, remember your survival instinct. This means protecting yourself and not being trapped by employers who don't understand. Many factors need to be considered, such as your personality, family and financial situation, other job opportunities, legal factors, the bully and your employer.

Before you take any type of action against the bully, whether informal or formal, make sure that you are able to cope emotionally, intellectually and financially. It is extremely distressing to have to fight for your job and self-respect. Always use the support and advice of trusted friends, col-leagues, and professionals such as a therapist, lawyer or general practi-tioner. You need to save yourself first. Your gut instinct is your safety sensor. Employ this natural safety device to help and protect yourself at each step along the way.

Tip 1: Manage the bullying immediately

The first time and place to start managing a bully is the moment when the bullying is happening or as soon as possible afterwards. The best way to block a bully's mean or abusive statement is by using a harmless comment, humorous joke or neutral retort. This takes away their power without threatening them. Deep down in their unconscious mind, they'll feel a twinge of embarrassment but nothing else. Your goal is to force them to respect you and back off. You could just smile pleasantly and say:

- 'Thanks for the feedback.'
- 'And … ?'
- 'Forgive me for speaking while you were interrupting.'
- 'I hope I'm not invisible?'

If you have the confidence to face your bully with a polite, firm, calm manner, then this is one of the safest ways to arrest their aggression. Bullies are less likely to attack when involved in a neutral conversation, without an obvious power difference. Don't reveal any anxiety or anger, as this will trigger their own survival instinct and they will feel threatened and spring back in retaliation. When you confront the bully in conversation or anyone else about your dislike of being bullied, be sensitive to the exact nature of their response. Are they committed to finding an equitable solution and prepared to accept that you felt bullied, regardless of their own perceptions? Are they willing to change the situation so you feel safe at work? If at any stage you detect their response is not fair, sympathetic and action-orientated, then you're likely in saltwater crocodile territory and you will need to protect yourself. Be wary of making any of your own threats and don't allow yourself to be further provoked. Here are some options when faced with a bullying response to your attempt at a constructive conversation:

- Apologise for how you challenged them, not what you said: ' I'm sorry if I annoyed you when I got frustrated and …'

- Find the cause: 'Are you angry because I got upset when you changed my shift?' 'Do you complain about my work because you think older people are less competent?'

- Specify bullying behaviours: 'I don't know what I've done to make you upset at me.' 'Are you aware that you're leaving me out of the email loop?' 'I'm upset when you gossip about me and undermine my reputation.'

- Provide solutions: 'When you humiliate me, I'm stressed for hours. I'd like you to stop.' 'We seem to have a difficulty, how can we resolve it?' 'What else do I need to do so that you will allow me to get on with my work?'

- Write a private, confidential letter to the bully setting out clear statements such as those above.

- If you feel capable of doing so, jokingly confront the bully and stun them with a retort: 'Congratulations, you're an excellent tyrant!' 'Do you want a medal for intimidating everyone?' 'Bully for bullies!'

Tip 2: Ask for informal assistance

If you're too scared to confront the bully directly, an informal approach with some assistance is a good tactic. You should find someone internally or externally who is competent, respected or designated to intervene and attempt to construct a resolution. Fellow employees with power to confront bullying may include your line manager, HR staff, employee assistance officer, occupational health and safety officer/representative, equity or sexual harassment officer, or trade union representative. Sometimes they may be a co-worker who has earned respect within the organisation.

The aim is to approach the bully in an assertive, nonthreatening manner in order to persuade them to behave respectfully without formal sanctions or investigation. To help the process you need to work out what you want to say and bring a written summary of the basic points to your colleague; for example, 'I'm being bullied by X. The bullying behaviour compromises my work. It's affecting my productivity and others are affected too. This is what I tried to do to stop being bullied. Here's my evidence. Can you help?' Your support person should be someone who speaks calmly and logically and won't threaten anyone. They should attend all your meetings with the bully.

When attending an informal meeting about the bullying, you need to behave in a calm, credible and rational manner. You need to provide evidence of the bully's behaviours. The organisation will respect your version as long as it isn't riddled with anger and blame. Honestly share how you feel about being bullied — 'I shake inside when he screams'; 'I am so distressed that I vomit on the way to work' — while showing some empathy towards the bully; for example, 'He's under pressure, and maybe doesn't realise what his shouting does to people'.

You might like to bring some literature to the meeting that supports your description of workplace bullying and the destructive impact on employees and companies. If the bullying is suddenly labelled by your superiors or the bully himself as a performance management issue, then you can challenge that description by bringing evidence of previous positive performance feedback reviews and other career successes. Request explicit written evidence of poor performance, don't accept hearsay. If in fact your work performance has reduced lately then offer an explanation as to why it occurred; for example, 'I never made mistakes that required this type of performance feedback until he began bullying me and I reported it', or 'Her bullying has affected my concentration. There is clear evidence that this can occur with victims of workplace bullying'. You can also use previous good performance reviews to show how the bullying affected your productivity.

Be aware that some managers may react negatively to this type of informal approach to workplace bullying by retaliating immediately with disciplinary action or a negative performance appraisal, though they will deny any motive of revenge. Confer with your support person about how to thwart this approach if you believe your manager is likely to act this way. Investigate if your local employment legislation provides adequate protection from victimisation as a result of making a properly founded complaint.

Always remember when talking about workplace bullying to be as clear and informative as possible. A good guide to help you explain to management your side of the story comes from researchers at Arizona State University.[1] They say to tell a story:

- with a clear beginning, middle and end
- that clearly identifies the bully
- that focuses on the bad behaviour of the bully, not the target
- with specific details about the bullying experiences, not other complaints
- that can anticipate and meet potential objections by acknowledging others' perspectives
- that vividly conveys the cost of the abuse, yet is not so emotional that the listener must console rather than work towards solving the problem
- that is consistent, with details of quotations, times, places and people.
- that uses metaphors or examples that others may find familiar
- that includes references to other people who have been bullied
- that provides details about the negative effects of bullying on peers and workplace productivity
- that paints the target as a survivor, not a victim
- that identifies what action the target took to address the behaviour.

Tip 3: Play the waiting game

> *Diana is a quietly spoken, capable executive who worked her way up the ladder to just under the glass ceiling. When she was given the task of restructuring a major department, the bullying began. A senior executive sabotaged her well-deserved promotion to the board, wanting a mate appointed instead. Her fellow executives were too scared to rock the boat and they sacrificed her for their 'boys' club'. Without an effective company mechanism for justice or a fair hearing she knew any attempt at challenging the situation would have fostered further victimisation. Instead she spent her time surviving the politics, avoiding confrontations at work, and ensuring her career remained unaffected. When she finally left, she was seen as improving her career, not someone who couldn't handle the tough business world.*
>
> *Mary is a psychologist who was bullied by less qualified colleagues. Each time they bullied her she challenged their errors and refused to complete inappropriate tasks. Sometimes it felt like a game of chess and other times it felt like 'cat and mouse'. Eventually their power evaporated and they ran out of steam to bully her.*

Sometimes the risk of confronting the bully and taking on your organisation is too high. You can be ostracised as a troublemaker and for upsetting the status quo. Your career can suffer. It's sometimes safer to put up with the bullying by blocking its more negative effects on you and then moving on later. Just like living with political oppression, it may be wise to do nothing, cruise along and play the waiting game. While you are waiting, the situation may change — the bully may leave, management may intervene, or another target may be in a better position to confront the bully. In the meantime you might also use some sick leave to take a break. The point here is to exit when you are ready. When using the waiting step, you must release your fear and anger so that you don't become paralysed while working near the bully. You need to protect your health, block the bullying and complete your minimum work responsibilities.

Try to avoid any conflict or being anywhere close to the bully. If you have to meet, aim for email or phone meetings. Conduct face-to-face meetings standing up, as they take less time. Try to meet in public or take a witness with you if you have to go into their office, then make it as brief as possible. While you are being abused, try to remain neutral. If you feel emotional tension beginning to rise, use some nonthreatening distracting activities — such as wiggling your toes, massaging your finger joints, blowing your nose, polishing your glasses, or cleaning your desk. If you feel overwhelmed at any time you are with them, use stomach problems as an excuse to go to the bathroom. You can also confuse your bully and blunt their attacks early by being unpredictable when you cross their path. You might be friendly one day, neutral or cold the next. Sometimes you say 'Hello' and sometimes not. If you can't avoid engaging them in social conversation, try to use nonwork topics to say something nice — for example, 'I do like your outfit'; or something confrontational — for example, 'I don't think that Carlton are playing at all well this season'.

Tip 4: Use friendly flattery

You can't always stay out of your bully's way, so you need to be prepared when he catches you for a bout of bullying. This is where you can use your natural survival instinct. Think about if you are caught speeding in your car. You're more likely to be as agreeable as possible than challenge the traffic police, as you can be sure it will avoid you getting into further trouble. Likewise if you don't threaten your bully, you're more likely to receive better treatment. In fact you can even try and manipulate the situation to extend the bully's behaviour away from threats and abuse and into a more favourable treatment of his 'target'. Superficial socialising to butter up and stay in favour with your bully can diminish a bullying situation. Although it may feel internally repulsive, regard it as a survival tactic or relabel it as 'killing them with kindness'. Your reward is your career, health and wellbeing. Flattering tactics to use include:

- Showing concern: 'You look tired, can I bring you a coffee?'
- Showing interest in the bully's personal life — their family, holidays, hobbies.
- Discussing areas of common interest; for example, sport, fashion, movies.
- Stroking their ego with personal and professional compliments; for example, 'I heard that your presentation went very well', 'Thanks for your suggestions, they will be extremely useful', ' I can't do this without your help'.
- Bringing in cookies for coffee breaks; giving birthday cards, flowers, and gifts on appropriate occasions.

Playing the waiting game

- *Be friendly to everyone, chitchat about neutral topics.*
- *Blend in with the crowd and don't stand out.*
- *Don't confront, challenge or threaten.*
- *Pretend to be placatory, subservient and give them the power.*
- *Use a bland, neutral expression with bullies.*
- *Don't cower or over-react.*
- *Hide any tears as well as possible and release your feelings later.*
- *Focus upon other things; for example, hobbies, your future.*
- *Hide your competencies and disguise your achievements.*
- *Don't reveal personal information which can be used against you.*
- *Don't make the bully jealous of your clothes, belongings or enjoyable private life.*

- Thanking the bully on a regular basis.
- Being impressed when they boast about important contacts and achievements.
- Asking unprompted for feedback to improve your work performance.
- Asking their advice about nonwork matters such as holidays, car purchase or financial matters.

Tip 5: Protect your finances

Most people use their income to live, pay their mortgage and save for retirement. This makes it very hard to leave a permanent job, particularly one that is convenient or enjoyable, apart from the bullying. You need to seriously consider your financial alternatives if you are forced to leave suddenly.

- Consider: sick leave, long service leave, retraining, or a move to another section.
- Research: income protection, workers compensation, government sickness or unemployment benefits, early retirement, and another job.
- Consult: a financial planner or accountant to look at refinancing your mortgage, reducing financial obligations, increasing superannuation, or finding emergency cash.

- Accept: that sometimes family and friends are only too willing to offer financial help for emergencies. Don't be proud, ask for it now.

Tip 6: Make a formal complaint

> *Bill's union helped him to prepare an official complaint, including writing down all the bullying behaviours. He submitted his complaint to the HR department, who had to investigate. Eventually he went to conciliation. He wasn't happy with the outcome because he'd been criticised, but was relieved the bully was made accountable.*

If your informal complaints fail, you can initiate a formal written complaint. Such a formal process should lead to an investigation by a designated authority, such as the HR department; or an external, experienced investigator, such as a lawyer or occupational psychologist. In theory, the process will provide a fair resolution for everyone, although as discussed previously the current lack of public and professional understanding of workplace bullying may make this process less than satisfying at present. Most dispute resolution professionals haven't had sufficient training in identifying workplace bullying or understanding its toxic impact. If the investigator, mediator or conciliator involved in your formal process appears to lack adequate training, their objectivity may be compromised and their sensitivity to targets may be lessened. This can mean that the whole formal process can cause more trauma for you. You need to think clearly and investigate properly before undertaking a formal complaint.

There are numerous options for the formal resolution of workplace conflicts and bullying. These vary according to various local legal structures and work cultures. A decision can be made using a form of mediation and conciliation which may in fact be regarded as being adversarial in some countries.[2] Mediation that is based upon an imbalance of power is generally unsuitable for bullying — for example, manager to employee — or when you are too traumatised to confront your bully. However, a collaborative process such as workplace conferencing (defined as a restorative practice) is far more effective. It creates a structured environment where everyone involved in the dispute moves from the past, to the present and then the future. Simultaneously, they shift their emotional state from conflict to cooperation, negotiation and finally, resolution.[3]

It is important that you investigate the professional integrity and value of the investigation and dispute resolution procedures that you will participate in, and you may need assistance to write your complaint and supply the relevant evidence. Use both professional feedback and your gut feelings to make a decision about the formal process and its usefulness to your situation. When you are required to attend any formal meetings bring along a supportive colleague, union representative or lawyer and ensure your own written record is made of all meetings, hearings and interviews.

You need to be prepared when undertaking a formal workplace bullying complaint to deal with criticism. Whether you are correctly or incorrectly accused of making mistakes, accept the feedback when appropriate; for example, 'I agree that I did …'; or dispute it logically and fairly — 'No, I disagree that I made a mistake, this is what I believe occurred …'. If possible provide compelling evidence that your version of events is the correct one. Remember that even if you did make mistakes at work they do not warrant bullying. You might say: 'Although I made some mistakes, it does not explain why he needed to bully me, when effective managers are expected to provide respectful, constructive feedback'. If in any formal meeting the battle is beginning to be based upon their word versus yours, use assertive body language, speak clearly and remain calm. Avoid the temptation to bite back if you feel they are taking cheap shots at you. Stick to the facts. People believe a confident person, not a scared, angry target!

Tip 7: Obtain legal or industrial support

> *In Australia, in a landmark decision, a bully and his employer, Ballarat Radio Pty Ltd, were convicted and fined by WorkSafe for bullying and failing to provide a safe workplace.*[4]

Although some people only consider the legal or industrial option as a last resort, I know of one Melbourne investigator of workplace disputes who uses a combination of local, state and federal legal avenues — industrial relations law, equal opportunity statutes, workers insurance procedures and occupational health and safety law. While such a complex approach isn't appropriate for everyone, you will need expert local legal advice (free or paid) to investigate the varied state and federal laws which may protect you from further bullying and provide some validation, justice or compensation.

If you are considering industrial action, then first find out if your union or professional association will intervene and take action. You may encourage your workmates to also approach them as witnesses or make a group complaint. Some states and countries now have appointed occupational health and safety workplace inspectors to whom you can complain separately. If considering legal avenues you will need specific advice from solicitors or lawyers working in the appropriate jurisdiction. The range of legal options in the criminal or civil courts is very wide. If you work for a multinational company, they may also operate under the laws of their country as well complying with local legislation. Always give your lawyer all your evidence and keep copies. And remember that while they are the experts in the law, you know the facts behind your case better than they do.

Examples of legislative avenues that may be relevant to workplace bullying include:

- equal opportunity, human rights, and antidiscrimination law
- occupational health and safety, and workers compensation law
- unfair and constructive dismissal legislation, and hostile work environment laws
- employment protection, and contract law
- industrial or workplace relations law
- common law claims for damages, negligence, or duty of care
- personal injury law
- antiretaliation statutes
- laws of natural justice
- liability (personal and vicarious)
- privacy law
- public sector ethics, freedom of speech and association
- malicious communication, and defamation law
- intentional infliction of nervous shock
- whistleblowing, and public-interest disclosure.

Tip 8: Report corrupt or criminal behaviours

Some employees use bullying behaviours to disguise unethical, illegal, fraudulent activities, which management may condone. If you suspect that is the case with your bully, then check with trusted colleagues and investigate further. You need to document all incriminating evidence before forwarding it to appropriate authorities; for example, the taxation department, government funding bodies, the board of directors, or a professional association. Areas to look at would be company policies and procedures, codes of conduct, mission statements, public relations material, annual shareholders reports, and board of management reports. Look for negligence, neglect of duty, malpractice, misappropriation of budgets (very common), financial irregularities, stealing, borrowing or losing clients' money, falsification of time sheets, pilfering, or breaches of rules and regulations. Other evidence may be reduced working hours, time wasted, cyber slacking, or unethical cyber use. Go as high as you can to find allies within your organisation — a manager, senior executive, board members or the chief executive officer — and investigate if the bully has other targets or witnesses who could testify or join a class action about the violations.

Bullies don't always realise that some work behaviours are criminal. If the bullying does involve criminal behaviour then it is best to report it to police. They will be in charge of the investigation, not the company. In some states you may be able to obtain a legal intervention order to stop such behaviour, but your workplace may retaliate. Examples of criminal behaviours include:

- assault, robbery, spraying with dangerous liquids, setting fires
- threatening phone calls and letters
- cyber bullying
- stalking, sexual abuse, harassment, rape
- fraud.

Tip 9: Go public

> Two lecturers were suspended without pay for 6 months because they objected publicly to a PhD thesis called 'Laughing at the Disabled' and placed a video of their complaint on YouTube.
>
> 'I appeared on national television, it was validating and liberating. They believed me! I was scared that I'd look like a victim but everyone said, "Good on you". I looked like a hero. Now it is out in the open I can move on.'

Because of the limited understanding of workplace bullying, the positive encouragement of further awareness within your organisation can be productive for both yourself and your fellow workers. The displaying of anti-discrimination policies and laws, recent articles on bullying, or business cards of workplace relations lawyers might be appropriate. You could also invite speakers — for example, a local doctor, a union representative, or a bullying expert — or attend workshops yourself and report back.

Alternatively you may wish to teach your company a lesson and go all out to put the matter in the eye of the general public. This is a serious step though, and one not to be undertaken lightly. You will need to keep your identity secret, unless you seek expert legal advice and are prepared to be subjected to a public barrage of attention, both good and bad, that can run totally out of your control. Your actions could backfire badly and hurt you. Most organisations prefer a good public profile and work hard to avoid negative public exposure. The law is impartial and no matter what your defence, if you commit a crime yourself such as defamation, you will face investigation and prosecution.

Some steps you can take to go public include:

- encouraging your union or colleagues to go public.

- purchasing company shares, and expressing your frustration at shareholders' meetings.

- forming a pressure group to lobby members of parliament.

- contacting the media; for example, talkback radio, newspaper journalists

- using your evidence to write about bullying in books, articles, internet sites.

Tip 10: Plan your exit

> 'Accept you're defeated. Get what you can and leave. I should have told them to fire me when the trouble began. They'd be forced to pay me out with a lot of money. Instead I tried to adapt and fit in. When I finally resigned it was less beneficial financially. I should have sought expert legal opinion. The best strategy for me was to get fired and get a settlement.'

Although the best solution for workplace bullying is for employers to resolve it with respect, many naive employers become adversarial and attack. For most targets the fight is not worthwhile. Thus, if you find yourself in a toxic workplace, it may be best to just move on. This means plan your exit now and don't wait for crumbs of justice that never materialise!

While some readers will gasp in horror at this suggestion, you may need to become more realistic. Although you think that you need or love your job, you can't sacrifice your health and everything else for it, nor should you think that if you leave, the bully has won. Eventually their bullying behaviours will boomerang back on them. Meanwhile you can move on to enjoy this life. Besides, when you're too injured to work, you could miss out on a better job!

While in some jurisdictions workers are able to sue for constructive or unfair dismissal when fired or forced to leave, it is best to seek legal advice to help you to assess the risks and remuneration associated with resigning as compared to being sacked. If you are confident of your emotional strength and career status, you may feel safe enough to confront your employer and gain a clearer picture of your options; for example, 'I don't like the way I'm being treated here. Are you trying to get rid of me?' 'If you want me to work here, why aren't you making it safe for me to fulfil my employment obligations?'

Tip 11: Deal with rehabilitation

> *Eva has met many rehabilitation consultants in her time, including the 'Sledgehammer'. She was pushed to retrain and return to work early while still severely traumatised and depressed. She was forced to take antidepressant medication (which produced bad side effects) under threat of the removal of her insurance income.*
>
> *Sarah couldn't return to her previous office job. She wanted to pursue her former love of making cosmetics. The insurer wouldn't pay for retraining. Her lawyer went to mediation. The insurance representative behaved like a secret service interrogator, but her claim was eventually approved. Sarah found this very validating.*

Some employees are not greatly injured by their workplace bullying and can take a brief time off and quickly return to their workplace or find work elsewhere. Others require long-term treatment or rehabilitation. The extent of rehabilitation services available for workers varies greatly across the world, from clinics or day hospitals to hourly rehabilitation consult-ants, often employed by profit-making companies. The standard of such care naturally also varies greatly. Unfortunately many organisations, insur-ance companies and independent rehabilitation providers don't have the compassion, knowledge, professional training or resources to provide a comprehensive, empathic rehabilitation service for bullying victims. Though some consultants may be caring, your recovery process may be limited by brief consultancy periods, lack of training, immaturity, inexperience and poor supervision. Rehabilitation professionals without medical training may impose medical treatment while ignoring other suitable forms of treatment — for example, yoga, massage or meditation. If you refuse such treatment, your financial payments may be suspended. It is therefore important that you look carefully at the rehabilitation offered to you by your employer and seek advice outside work on ways to access the best rehabilitation services for your individual needs.

Employee insurance schemes or government services may provide vocational training programs and services to assist injured employees back to work, retrain perpetrators and offer retraining for those forced to leave. In addition to vocational retraining, assertiveness skills and psychological therapy, you may require extras such as weight reduction and physical exercise. If you encounter difficulties with your employer's insurance company providing appropriate assistance, then you may need to take legal measures to obtain the skills you require to return to work. As with all legal processes, however, this can be stressful so you need to obtain proper professional advice regarding treatment and retraining. You do not want inadequate rehabilitation processes to exacerbate your injuries and retard your return to work.

Tip 12: Make your next job count

> 'On the fourth day of my new job the boss's secretary said that she wanted to see me. I was so scared I began to shake, but when I walked in she told me what an excellent job I was doing. Now I'm working very hard, feeling creative and talented. Despite long hours I don't notice the clock. I still can't hear the name of my former bully without feeling ill, but that'll go in time. I manage 10 people now. The key to my successful management style is to do the opposite of how my previous bullying manager would do it!'

> Whenever Tina thought of applying for another job she could hear her bully in her head screaming, swearing and accusing her, 'You're no good, nobody will hire you'.

Today's employees are changing careers numerous times and working in a number of different jobs during their lifetime. Many find that as one door closes another one opens. Similarly, you may find it easy to obtain a similar job or prefer a new career. If your bullying experience has, however, been particularly traumatic you may feel burnt out, stuck with painful memories, a lack of opportunities, and be suffering from your previous employer blackening your reputation and refusing to provide a reference. While this may make the next step hard, if you follow a positive program of preparation and commitment you can begin again. This involves obtaining professional career advice and investigating alternative careers, as well as rebuilding your confidence and refreshing your job seeking skills. A simple career formula based upon investigation and adjustment includes:

- current employment opportunities
- your qualifications
- your interests, skills, personality (as affected by trauma)
- other recent difficulties; for example, physical difficulties.
- family and environmental factors.

Although many jobs are advertised, there's a saying that claims 80% of jobs are not actually advertised. You could be competing with every other jobseeker who can't use their network or 'cold call' future employers. Thus explore the hidden job market as well. Consult career consultants, vocational psychologists, employment agencies or experienced rehabilitation consultants for assistance as well as researching newspaper and internet sites. Don't be afraid to knock on doors, talk to friends, colleagues, clients or anyone with employment connections. To help get you back into work shape try learning a new hobby, doing voluntary or part-time work, or finding a less demanding role at first to build your confidence. Get help with your curriculum vitae and touch up your job interview skills by practising with someone trusted or by yourself to a video recorder. Try to be animated and passionate — wear a 'confident mask' to hide your unconfident self and develop some practice answers to standard interview questions; for example, 'Why did you leave your last job?' 'How do you handle difficulties — give examples?' 'What sort of work were you proud about?' 'What are your strengths and weaknesses?'

When preparing your approach to the job market, explore the issues below to sharpen your focus:

- Can you return to your previous career or do you need something less stressful?
- What job opportunities or new careers are available?
- What are your professional strengths and weaknesses, training and experience?
- How easily can you transfer your skills to another career?
- Have you achieved other successes which can create new directions; for example, turning a hobby into a career?
- Do you require further training?
- Do you need help to develop stronger boundaries at work to protect yourself and block any future bullying?
- Do you have dreams which may lead you in a new direction, such as a sea change?
- If you would prefer to be self-employed, what could you do?

If you have been forced out of your job without a reference, future employers and employment agencies may use this against you, thus it is vital you are prepared to combat this. At the very least you can request a statement of service from your former employer that covers your roles, responsibilities and dates. If you are worried your previous employer will provide a bad verbal reference, ask a friend to act as if they are a prospective employer and phone your previous employer to check out what they say about you. You can also use earlier references, testimonials from satisfied clients or former work colleagues. Make sure you obtain new references from any recent voluntary or part-time work you have been doing.

When attending a job interview be sure to find out if it is a new position and if not, why your predecessor left. Check out the work environment — is it quiet or fun? Is the layout isolated offices or open plan? Is it an attractive working environment? Are lunch facilities provided? While being interviewed remember to show respect for the organisation and find out what they do to build staff culture and improve management skills. Assess their reaction when you ask how they handle conflict (or bullying) and find out who can mentor you when you feel uncertain. It is important to be as clear as possible about the culture of your new workplace. Just as an employee with a physical handicap requires ramps and lifts, similarly you need a psychologically safe workplace. If you have a bad gut feeling, don't take the next job without psychological coaching. Not only is it awful to be bullied again but your ability to survive at work will be affected. You may be able to check other sources of information about your future employer on websites, business magazines or industry grapevines.

Throughout the entire return-to-work process it is important to watch out for bullying voices in your head that can undermine your progress to a new and satisfying job. There are three main types of feedback: negative, constructive, and positive. If you keep hearing your bully's malicious voice and have lost self-confidence, then find some respected, competent colleagues or coaches. Ask them for their own feedback on your work ethic, competencies and personality to help you improve or negate nasty criticisms. If you find that your bullying experience has left you too cynical, you may be suspicious of any new workplace and unable to trust. This kind of thinking can poison your relationships with good people, who will see you as negative, difficult, paranoid or arrogant. You need to be strong enough to recognise what your inner self is doing to your prospects of a happy work life and find professionals who can help you rebuild your self-esteem and relate to other employees with confidence.

Tip 13: To tell or not to tell — that's the dilemma!

Many targets aren't sure what to tell a future employer when they are inevitably asked why they left their previous job. Some feel ashamed, others fear that they won't get the job if a future employer knows that they have been bullied, and others realise it looks bad to criticise a previous employer. The decision is a personal one but best based on how you feel about calmly and nondefensively explaining the situation and your own emotional and physical reactions. Remember that bullying can scramble your interview skills, so don't present like a victim and do dress for success! If you choose to tell, don't censure your previous workplace, just reframe the circumstances, making it clear how the bully's behaviour affected your ability to work productively for your employer and how you regretfully had to leave a job you liked before the bullying. Be constructive, relate your challenges in a positive manner, and validate your search for a better job. Everyone respects employees who confront serious challenges but move on.

Alternatively, if you choose not to tell then you will have to find a convincing answer to the employer's question of why you left your previous job. It is recommended though that you eventually disclose the events that

Do's	and Don'ts
• Communicate effectively to others	• Remain silent
• Be flexible and adaptable	• Deny feedback about your role
• Get support, inform senior managers	• Alienate people who can support you
• Confront the bully if safe	• Expect the bully to improve by osmosis
• Keep accurate records	• Hope it won't happen again
• Find out your legal rights	• Blame yourself or feel guilty
• Question the bully and organisation	• Trust the bully support gang
• Protect yourself	• Neglect yourself and be injured
• Accept that you work to live	• Believe that you live to work
• Become emotionally strong to confront the situation	• Stay stuck and do nothing
• Maintain adequate work performance	• Pay back by working less
• Be prepared for the next bully attack	• Wait for their empathy to work
• Take time off	• Stay and aggravate your injury
• Consider your options to move on	• Remain a victim

occurred at your previous workplace once you have been employed; otherwise, if something goes wrong, you may be treated unfairly.

Possible approaches to take to the issue of your next job can be summarised into some possible themes:

- *Positive:* 'I needed time off for other things.'
- *Honest:* 'I was harassed until I decided enough was enough and left.'
- *Realistic:* 'I couldn't achieve my career goals in a toxic culture.'
- *Blame:* 'I loved my job but my doctor (or psychologist) told me to leave.'
- *Ambitious:* 'I clashed with a culture of incompetence.'
- *Creative:* 'The climate changed and I didn't like what was happening.'

Tip 14: Learn to deal with bullying at a new workplace

> Bonnie went from the frying pan into the fire. The moment she began, she realised that there was just as much bullying at the new job. She backs off, blocks their toxic impact and laughs.

> Hans swore he'd never work for a bully again. But his future manager worked overseas so he couldn't obtain references. During the job interview he had a gut feeling, but listened to his rational side and took the job. Three months later, he regretted his decision. At first his boss seemed pleasant, but he was a Dr Jekyll and Mr Hyde character. He could praise, denigrate or contradict himself. He set impossible goals and lacked business ethics. He sacked so many people there weren't enough left to cover the amount of work that was required. He dismissed Hans a few weeks after he'd made him permanent. Eventually Hans went into his own business.

> When Sarah returned to work, she found it difficult to begin again. She was more sensitive, wary and found it hard to trust others. She felt as though her brain had a corrupted file in it and it affected her ability to cope.

Although bullying can occur in any workplace, it's more likely to occur in certain industries than others. Therefore when moving to a job in a similar field, you should assess whether or not your bullying experiences are likely to be repeated. Although you may be pleased to be employed and working again, you will feel far worse if you can't cope with high stress levels or bullying in your next job. Be aware that if you encounter regular bullying behaviours in your new job towards yourself or others, this might inadvertently remind you of your previous bully and stir up bad memories. This can increase the chances that you might react inappropriately and exacerbate the bullying. Hopefully this feeling will soon dissolve but these painful memories should act as your warning sensor. If you start to feel similar emotional and physical symptoms to the last time you were bullied, obtain immediate professional support. Consult your psychologist to learn how to deal with the distress, deploy some bully blocking techniques, or start to plan another departure. Take action to protect yourself.

CHAPTER TEN

Beware the medico–legal hazards

> ❝*Ruth is an attractive woman in her mid-40s, with a loving and supportive family. She enjoyed working in the welfare sector, and managed over 40 unruly staff. A new manager was appointed and began a campaign of bullying. Ruth was forced to work longer hours until her physical and emotional health broke down. When she reported the bullying things became worse. Management forced her staff to turn against her, even though she had never received any prior disciplinary or performance warnings. An external investigator was brought in and when the allegations against her couldn't be substantiated, the investigation abruptly ceased! When she finally applied for workers' compensation they questioned her professional credibility, her privacy was invaded, and her rights eroded. She was suspected of fraud even though she hadn't done anything wrong. During a subsequent court case she discovered that her employer had been conducting surveillance on her for over 6 months. She had been videotaped at home through her kitchen window and going out to appointments. Her privacy complaint was settled at mediation. Seven years later, she began some voluntary work, which turned into a real job. Her compensation case still hasn't been heard in court, nor has she received validation.* ❞

Some people who have been injured by workplace bullying are fortunate to have automatic access to professional support, often through their employer or their insurer. Others are far less fortunate, they may decide to initiate legal proceedings against their employer for offences such as salary, medical expenses, wrongful dismissal, discrimination, or abuse of natural justice. If this applies to you, then you will need to prove that you were bullied, or wrongly accused of bullying, based on legal evidence and witness statements, which may be hard to obtain as many witnesses fear for their job and will not turn against their employer. You may also need to prove that your injury is a medically diagnosed consequence of the bullying, and that you are not malingering.

The adversarial nature of the legal system means that this process will force you to wage a battle against those who want to prove that there is insufficient legal evidence that the bullying actually occurred, or that your injuries were pre-existing or caused by other factors, and therefore not related to the bullying. This battle will be fought regardless of the strength of your perception and experience of being bullied. Thus, while pursuing your right to justice, treatment, compensation, rehabilitation and validation, you will need to negotiate a maze of medico–legal hazards along the way. These include the people and processes involved with the law, medicine and psychology, as well as your employer, investigation, rehabilitation and insurance companies. The same hazards can also apply if you have been accused of bullying, whether correctly or incorrectly. Your best defence against this minefield is to be prepared and know what can happen.

The compensation system

> Annette's employer was then the only one in the country to be fined for having an unsafe workplace due to bullying. Yet when she reported her bullying at another location, they denied it. She was further injured by being forced out without a reference or unemployment benefits. Her employer's insurance company paid for medical expenses but she had to go to court to obtain her financial entitlements and some validation. She and her husband needed an income to cover expenses, and were eventually forced to sell the family home.

When you are too injured to work you will generally require a salary and medical treatment. Depending upon the employment laws where you live, some costs may be covered by your employer's insurance. Although you may need this financial assistance, you may have a realistic fear of the stigma and shame it can bring. Insurance companies often listen to your employer and may refute your claim for salary, medical and allied benefits. This means you will need a lawyer and if possible, your union, to challenge their denial. As discussed previously, you may make your complaint alone or encourage other targets to join a class action. Beware that by taking some action you may also pressure their insurance company to hold your employer financially accountable, through increased premiums and/or other legal avenues such as fines.

Medico–legal interviews

When Jenny faced medico–legal examinations, she agonised about forgetting important details. She was still slashing her arms regularly at that stage. She found it difficult to eat and sleep for two nights before an interview. We wrote down her symptoms and the impact of the bullying on her life. At the next interview, she gave her list to the doctor. She worried less and the doctor had more detail.

You may need to expose your personal story many times to a new doctor, therapist, medico–legal assessor, human resources staff, lawyer or investigator during informal and formal meetings. These interviewers will follow their agenda of questions, which will probably not include your whole experience. Thus although it could be healing to have your story identified and recorded, the anticipation of the appointment can be very stressful; you may be afraid that you will forget important details, and worry about the quality of the interview process you are forced to undergo. In addition, being pressured to recall extremely painful experiences many times over can release disturbing, intense memories that trigger symptoms such as tears, panic attacks and nightmares. The toxic effect of a poor interview can affect you for ages.

Although any interview is stressful, even when you are assessed in a fair, ethical and sensitive manner, by a skilled, respectful interviewer who has had training in understanding workplace bullying, it can be extremely disabling and humiliating to constantly repeat your story in new, uncomfortable environments. This becomes even more traumatic when the interviewer has limited time or appropriate professional expertise to build respect and rapport with you, and obtain the information they require without further threatening you.

The following tips for dealing with interviews will help guide you through the process:

• Bring a brief summary of several pages. Include what happened at work and subsequent events. Bring evidence about your past work performances and any witness statements, as well as feedback from others about your personality before and after the bullying — for example, *Jackie is a friendly, efficient employee.* An earlier photo of you and a list of your previous social activities might also help.

- Summarise your injuries, including physical, psychological, and cognitive; the damage to your career, self-esteem, social life and family relationships; financial consequences; the medication you have been prescribed; and anything else relevant, such as job applications, rejections, or requests for management help.

- Ask if you can bring a support person with you to the interview. If you are refused, then seek assistance from your doctor, lawyer or union about this.

- Ask prior permission to use a tape recorder; their refusal may suggest that there is something to hide.[1] Alternatively, review the interview process and behaviours as they occur and write them down. If queried by the interviewer then use your poor memory as a reason.

- If you are feeling extremely threatened at any time during an interview, leave and tell them why.

- Be aware that all information — personal or work-related — can be misinterpreted and used against you, so obtain advice about exactly what to say. When asked questions about your personal life, give minimal detail and focus on your work-related experiences and injury.

- Make sure that anyone who writes a report has access to all your information, not just the material supplied by your employer. It may help to ask them for a list of what they have been given by the insurer.

- Be careful about the level of authority over medical matters that you give your employer, their insurance company, doctors, psychologists or lawyers. Read all consent material carefully and include a requirement that 'Only written information relating to my compensatable injury is to be accessed'. Only sign forms with which you totally agree, or when you have received legal advice that there is no other option. You may be able to revoke permission at times, such as when you signed under duress or without the opportunity to seek legal counsel.

- Investigate privacy laws and/or freedom of information laws to obtain copies of phone calls, emails, memos, and all reports written about you by medical experts, employers and insurance companies. This information will be necessary for any protracted legal battles. Your lawyer or general practitioner may assist.

Medico–legal assessments

> Dina's claim for workplace bullying was accepted 8 years ago. Since then, the insurer has forced her to see many psychiatrists for assessments. Some showed no understanding of workplace bullying. One psychiatrist's questions reminded Dina of being back in the bully's office, feeling terrified, interrogated as to why she'd left her previous job 19 years earlier and taken a pay cut to work in a beautiful setting. She felt humiliated for being single. Dina had bought a flat shortly before her breakdown then let it immediately and sold it for a profit soon after. The psychiatrist's report mentioned that flat 23 times, suggesting that this caused Dina's distress, not the bullying. Dina believes that the psychiatrist manipulated Dina's words to create doubt in the insurer's mind. She made sure she obtained new assessments for herself later on.

Medico–legal assessments are used to establish your injuries, validity of treatment programs and monitor them. You can be interviewed many times by different psychologists or psychiatrists. Although psychological reports are used occasionally, legal systems generally prefer psychiatric assessments. Be aware that psychiatrists are trained by medical psychiatric systems to investigate individual psychiatric disorders and personalities, not systemic organisational abuse. They do not assess anyone else in the bullying situation, including the bully, the managers, or bystanders; nor do they investigate and assess the organisational culture, quality of leadership and other relevant work factors.

Many other mental health professionals conducting assessments do not obtain an adequate history of your personal and work life, or assess the crucial impact of bullying upon your social and cultural environment and whether or not the bullying has disabled your day-to-day life. Others blame incidents in your past for your difficulties, instead of assessing your symptoms and actual workplace experiences.

Some mental health professionals blame your personality, even though there is no evidence of a general victim personality at work.[2] A diagnosis of personality disorder can only be made when there is clear evidence of it dating back to childhood or adolescence, and when the person's history indicates psychopathological difficulties or early temperamental problems.[3] Unless your personality was assessed before the bullying began or other relevant clinical evidence has been made available, you should not be diagnosed with a prior condition. Only your current injuries can be assessed.

There is sufficient research evidence showing that trauma can severely alter some personalities. Heinz Leymann, the pioneer of studies on workplace bullying in Sweden and Germany, believes that because chronic bullying alters the personality and thus there is no such thing as a pre-morbid personality.[4] Nevertheless, you can be blamed and seen as malingering, overreacting or fabricating. Assessments may ignore the possible impact of earlier traumas that can exacerbate your injuries, for example, earlier sexual assault leading to cumulative trauma. This prior trauma can be entirely different to a workplace bullying injury and in these cases, the causes of each symptom need to be assessed.

It is important to investigate or distinguish between causality or causal links. You can have several physical health problems (e.g., a stomach virus and arthritis) or a number of unrelated psychological difficulties (e.g., mourning an elderly parent's death, and bullying) simultaneously and a variety of symptoms . Yet many mental health professionals don't always investigate and check out any correlation between the bullying and recent physical disorders — for example, putting on weight, higher blood pressure, thyroid disorders, auto-immune disorders, skin disorders. Many also ignore recent research into what are termed relational disorders, involving two or more people. Relational disorders are serious behavioural disturbances that can lead to major impairments in physical health and psychological adjustment.[5]

Although some people are more vulnerable to stress and depression, many professionals forget that a trauma is an abnormal event. It can be devastating to anyone, and severely alter and injure a normal, healthy personality. Proper history-taking should reveal whether or not a target's life felt threatened, whether by subtle social stigma or direct physical threats.

At present, there is no psychiatric diagnosis for workplace bullying trauma, and many create diagnoses without reference to the American Psychiatric Association's *Diagnostic and Statistical Manual of Mental Disorders* (DSM IV), an accepted international diagnostic system developed by committees of experienced mental health professionals.[6] Although mental health professionals may feel restricted by the current lack of diagnosis for bullying injuries, they can still validate victims in their reports by describing them as 'traumatised', instead of normalising bullying and implying that targets cannot cope with everyday stressors, or blaming them with inappropriate labels such as 'adjustment disorder'.

Poor professional integrity

> *Lila was sent to the insurer's psychologist for an assessment. His report blamed her for the problems. Then she discovered that the insurer had only sent documentation of their own position ahead of the interview and neglected to send any of Lila's evidence supporting her claim, despite it all being on file. When she finally faxed her evidence through, the psychologist revised his report and supported her claim.*

Many mental health professionals who may be called upon by insurers to assess and report on a suspected case of workplace bullying are oblivious to the current research on workplace bullying trauma. They have not read the literature, attended conferences or undertaken professional development on the many pitfalls the field holds for both professionals and clients. Their reports risk corruption when pressured by employers and insurers. Many whistleblowers are exposed to an unethical alliance between entrepreneurial psychiatrists looking for new income opportunities and corrupt management systems looking for new victims to blame.[7] Some mental health professionals turn to medico–legal assessments to top-up their superannuation pile, whereas others reduce long-term patients in favour of a less structured practice. A few become too loyal to their sponsors, while some rely upon their age and reputation to disguise their lack of knowledge about workplace bullying. Thus, sadly, some professional dinosaurs can do a lot of damage.

A further problem arises when mental health professionals have blind spots and forget that many strange, nasty people go to work, including sociopathic bullies. Psychiatrist Jean Linnane remarked that 'Many psychiatrists have forgotten their ethical obligations. They've screamed, abused and harassed victims'.[8] Psychologist April Harper notes further that every day 'injured human beings are held accountable for behaviours and personalities of persons who don't exist save in the mind of the reporting psychiatrist. They can totally destroy your career and financial security'.[9]

Dealing with dodgy interviews

> 'I was warned by my support group that Dr X was arrogant and aggressive. They were right. So I wrote to the Medical Board asking if his behaviours were standard practice. They replied saying that he'd behaved appropriately! Soon after, another one from our group was forced to see him. Guess what? Suddenly he was caring and considerate.'

If you believe that you were unfairly treated or did not receive a fair hearing when you were interviewed, then you, your doctor, union or lawyer can take action to explain your distress or request procedural information. Any query about the interview style must been done immediately after your interview, long before you receive their report. Otherwise, your complaints may be interpreted as anger at the report's findings. Later on, if you disagree with the report, investigate further action to obtain a more accurate assessment. Your union or lawyer may be able to challenge the report and request an assessment from someone else. The following options provide a guide to dealing with questionable interview practices:

- You can write to the referral organisation, such as the insurance company and/or the state licensing authority or professional association. Your role is to encourage them to investigate the interviewer's professional practices and initiate learning opportunities for them to understand and treat victims of bullying with respect. Generally I would encourage you to provide polite, constructive feedback about their behaviours. Don't retaliate because of their lack of understanding.

- You can write to seek clarification and inquire why certain questions were considered relevant to a workplace injury; for example, 'Do you dye your hair?' 'Why didn't you marry?' 'I see that your partner is black?'

- Request the research evidence demonstrating the validity of their line of questioning (e.g., 'Do you have a sex life?') or decisions you made, (e.g., 'Why didn't you leave?') is valuable in making this medico–legal assessment.

- Inquire as to whether you could obtain the list of symptoms that formed their diagnosis.

- Inquire about the theoretical basis used to assess whether or not your symptoms were consistent with a trauma or other injuries caused by workplace bullying.

- Inquire about the training and experience of the interviewer in understanding and treating employees injured by workplace bullying.

- Inquire whether the behaviours of your employer, manager, bullies, witnesses and dysfunctional work systems were assessed.

Diagnostic difficulties

An effective mental health diagnostician's role is to assess all the physical and psychological symptoms presented by a patient before making a diagnosis. In the case of an employee injured by workplace bullying these victims may be suffering several diagnosable conditions, including severe depression, anxiety, panic attacks and trauma. It is the diagnosis related to trauma, however, that is the one that particularly requires further research, as it appears to take on a significant role in changing personalities and destroying lives. Many victims may qualify for a diagnosis of posttraumatic stress disorder but remain undiagnosed. They are further penalised and damaged because their bullying experiences are not regarded as traumatic, life-threatening or permanent. This has severe treatment, compensation and legal implications.

However, regardless of labels, if the workplace bullying has threatened your survival, you may be traumatised and suffer serious physical and psychological injuries that require treatment and future adjustment. Thus ultimately, any diagnosis needs to be very carefully considered and based upon all the presenting symptoms.

Posttraumatic stress disorder (PTSD)

Traumatic events include any threat, actual or perceived, to the life or physical safety of a person, their loved ones or those around them and lead to feelings of intense fear, helplessness or horror.[10]

While in the future medical science will no doubt develop sophisticated neurotransmitter testing for relevant hormones such as cortisol, serotonin and dopamine, or accurate brain scans, or something new to diagnose PTSD from a biochemical perspective,[11] in the meantime the criteria used for diagnosis are quite subjective. They change with each revised edition of the DSM. The current edition of the manual is the DSM-IV, while the DSM-V will be released in 2013. There is also the *ICD-10 Classification of Mental and Behavioural Disorders*[12] and the more recent *Psychodynamic Diagnostic Manual* (PDM, 2006).[13] Unfortunately these constructed diagnostic classifications are often allocated or rejected throughout a workplace bullying investigation without thorough examination by the medical diagnostician and then simultaneously used by lawyers and insurers as final verdicts to judge a victim's physical and mental condition! Never the less, there is mounting evidence that people who have suffered a serious case of workplace bullying are experiencing the major symptoms of PTSD.

Currently, the major criteria used to diagnose a posttraumatic stress disorder includes exposure to a single or sustained number of cumulative, frightening events, which cause physical injury, threaten one's physical integrity and are regarded as life-threatening.[14] It is implied that almost anyone would experience them as traumatic. Simultaneously, the person experiences extreme powerlessness and helplessness. They may subsequently re-experience the trauma regularly, avoid confronting it, or find ways to numb their pain. Their body reacts negatively to painful thoughts and memories. If you have experienced a physically life-threatening event and exhibit an appropriate number of symptoms from the major categories (re-experiencing, avoidance/numbing and hyperarousal) you may have a posttraumatic stress disorder or a chronic or complex posttraumatic stress disorder.[15]

In the case of workplace bullying, this is clearly a form of psychological and social violence that causes a variety of injuries. Currently there is worldwide disagreement among mental health professionals over whether victims of workplace bullying may also experience a posttraumatic stress disorder. The noted Swedish psychologist Heinz Leymann and others have demonstrated that PTSD can be an appropriate diagnosis for some workplace bullying victims; however, many psychiatrists and psychologists stick to the literal meaning of the disorder under the DSM-IV. Thus diagnoses differ according to the country, and sometimes victims are even diagnosed as having an adjustment disorder which experts such as Professors Alexander McFarlane and Gavin Andrews state can only be considered if they don't last longer than 6 months.

The critical issue is whether the sustained, emotional and abusive bullying experienced by a victim is the same as the threat of death or injury.[16] Can workplace bullying be identical to a life-threatening physical event? To consider this as true means that events and experiences such as the loss of physical and psychological health, social and family relationships, and career and tribal affiliations need to be considered as life-threatening.

Many researchers have explored the consequences of PTSD and neurological responses, and the effect of traumatic events. For example, there are major biochemical differences and physiological changes between chronic stress, depression and PTSD.[17] Research demonstrates that trauma causes physical and psychological injury. This has been shown by brain scans, saliva and blood cortisol tests. Victims with lower cortisol levels show evidence of PTSD. Thus being bullied may create psychological and physiological consequences.[18] In fact, brain scans and cortisol tests show that physical and social pain are similar in 'experience, function, and underlying neural structure'.[19]

Additionally, it has been found that the victim's perception of the trauma is a greater risk factor for trauma than objective ratings.[20] A 2009 study by Australian researcher Miranda Van Hooff and colleagues[21] into classifying an event as either traumatic (satisfying DSM-IV Criterion-A1 for PTSD) or nontraumatic (life event) raised doubts about the functionality of PTSD diagnostic criteria that appear to be influenced by the rater's subjective interpretation of them. In fact, many events classified as nontraumatic were associated with higher rates of PTSD.

Research into the effects of torture has also highlighted the role that nonphysical attacks have on a victim.[22] The 'internal experiences' that include being overwhelmed, sense of catastrophe, loss of sense of security, fears of injury and death in posttraumatic stress disorder are all dependent on the state of mind or cognitive structuring of the victim. Individual differences in affective, cognitive, somatic and relationship patterns together combine to create complex pictures as a consequence of traumatic events.[23]

Clearly then the current interpretation of the DSM-IV in relation to PTSD is restrictive and open to misinterpretation. Many health professionals understand and validate when there is trauma but diagnose within the defined limitations, whereas others do not understand or diagnose appropriately. Most use a diagnostic cocktail of adjustment disorder, generalised anxiety disorder, chronic stress, prolonged/persistent duress stress disorder (PDSD) or posttraumatic embitterment disorder (PTED).[24] The result is that many bullying victims who may qualify for a diagnosis of posttraumatic stress disorder remain undiagnosed. They are further penalised and damaged because their bullying experiences are not regarded as traumatic, life-threatening or permanent. This has severe treatment, compensation and legal implications.

The future does hold some hope however. *The Australian Guidelines for the Treatment of Adults with Acute Stress Disorder and Posttraumatic Stress Disorder: Practitioner Guide by the Australian Centre for Posttraumatic Mental Health* has now developed an empirically validated screening measure that applies to many victims of workplace bullying.[25] (In fact, recent Australian Medicare (2009) guidelines were published with a misprint, 'personal' threat was used instead of 'physical' threat — perhaps the editor is predicting future diagnostic criteria!) And it is thought by many in the field that the next edition of the DSM-V due out in 2013 will acknowledge workplace bullying as a possible cause of severe, chronic trauma.[26] However, our next challenge is to deal with the fact that the unique nature of workplace bullying appears to produce an identifiable set of symptoms.

Workplace bullying trauma (WBT)

'In victims of bullying, the symptoms of arousal and re-experience formed a single cluster of symptoms with avoidance remaining as a separate cluster'.[27]

The terms 'Holocaust survivor', 'victim of child sexual abuse' or 'survivors of political torture' indicate that not all traumas are the same. Biochemical research shows that males and females experience trauma differently.[28] There is also growing evidence of a unique cluster of symptoms experienced by victims of workplace bullying, similar to that experienced by rape victims.[29] Anyone who listens regularly to a victim obsessively recounting their experiences will identify exactly what this means. Yet currently, there is little systematic research-based evidence to support the concept of a new form of trauma. Thus, as we lack a suitable diagnosis, I believe that it is possible to identify a unique psychological condition resulting from the impact of workplace bullying and think that the time has come for this condition to be fully researched to identify its unique characteristics.

Thus, until we have clearer research-based evidence, I would like to propose that there are some victims of workplace bullying who may, in addition to other difficulties such as anxiety or depression, experience a specific form of trauma, namely, workplace bullying trauma (WBT). You can use this as a guideline to understand why you are so different now. In my experience, the symptoms, progress and treatment present differently to other forms of trauma. For example, in my experience, in most other trauma cases, such as those who have experienced child sexual abuse, domestic violence, or violent crime, the victims often repeat details while completing their story, sometimes long after the abuse has ended. They do not constantly obsess for years, and actually avoid repeating their story. In addition, even if they miss out on justice, they are more likely to receive some form of validation when the abuse is reported — for example, via a police report, or the media.

WBT symptoms checklist for seriously injured victims

- **Obsessive reviewing:** *A victim may constantly re-experience most events by obsessively reviewing segments and sections of their story in great detail, over and over, often for years.*

- **Fear and avoidance:** *The level of hypervigilance is extremely high in relation to actual bullying experiences (e.g., verbal bullying). Victims may have a paranoid fear of further attack and injustice. This is demonstrated by total social avoidance, such as not going shopping alone, answering the phone, or going outside to the letterbox.*

- **Projection:** *The fear of further abuse is displaced onto anyone associated with the bullying, including doctors, psychologists, lawyers, insurance clerks or neighbours. Targets may experience standard questions, unfortunate delays, unintentional mistakes, uncaring interviewers and bureaucratic behaviours as a direct continuation of the bullying, thereby becoming further injured.*

- **Ongoing consequences:** *Many workplace bullying victims experience their abuse as ongoing, especially when there are years of financial, legal, employment, health and personal issues that result from the bullying. Unlike many other victims of trauma, most targets appear able to recall more significant events or important aspects of the trauma.*

- **Panic attacks:** *Many victims experience seemingly unwarranted high levels of hyperarousal, anxiety and severe panic attacks when, for example, going into a shop or attending a social gathering.*

- **Social anxiety:** *Victims may develop a social fear or phobia as their previous social and family life deteriorates; they go out less socially and some even feel like social outcasts.*

- **Freezing:** *Many seriously injured victims are paralysed, stuck in their painful past, unable to mourn and move on, live in the present or prepare for the future. They describe themselves as being exhausted, spaced out, or stuck in time. Hours go past and they have little awareness of where time goes.*

(continued over)

WBT symptoms checklist for seriously injured victims *(continued)*

- **Personality implosion:** *Some victims demonstrate a disintegration of their personality and seem to implode, changing from coping, competent, social personalities into distressed, difficult, crushed or paralysed people.*

- **Long-lasting injury:** *Some victims have high levels of trauma, anxiety and depression for many years after leaving the irresponsible workplace, regardless of compensation payouts. They can remain injured for years, hopeless and powerless, unable to move on and rebuild their life.*

- **Common physical symptoms:** *These include hair loss, weight gain (often 20+ kilograms), speech difficulties and voice changes (e.g., one voice for describing prebullying experiences, another one for postbullying), sleep problems and nightmares.*

- **Difficulty focusing:** *Many victims have major problems concentrating or focusing on anything else, such as maintaining housework, cooking meals, gardening and paperwork, apart from the bullying and related issues.*

- **Public shame:** *Targets/victims often do not feel as though they have received any form of acknowledgment or public validation of their workplace bullying experiences. It may be excluded in the incident report, denied by the HR department because there is insufficient evidence, or left out of medical reports, despite the fact that some form of public validation is essential for healing and rebuilding their personality.*

- **Loss of confidence:** *Confidence, built up over many years prior may be lost in personal and professional abilities and engagement in other activities or hobbies may cease.*

Understanding local laws and legislation

> 'Understanding local laws and legislation. No one should be subjected to degrading treatment or punishment.
>
> No one should be subjected to attacks upon their honour and reputation.
>
> Everyone has the right to just and favourable conditions of work.'
>
> *Universal Declaration of Human Rights, 1948*

Even though you have the right to be treated fairly at work, if your human rights are not respected, then validation and justice are difficult. Legal definitions of bullying vary across the world and there are different legal options. In many countries — the United Kingdom, Australia, United States of America — there is no coherent approach. You will need to investigate your legal rights under a variety of criminal (e.g., the courts) and civil (e.g., industrial tribunals) jurisdictions, including provisions related to discrimination (sex, disability, race), personal injury, wrongful discharge, privacy, whistleblowing, negligence, and workplace safety. These vary according to your state, country and legal systems. The costs also vary, some being prohibitive for those out of work, unless they find a lawyer on the 'no win, no fee' basis. Even in progressive countries such as Scandinavia, excellent laws for tackling workplace bullying are difficult to enforce. For example, despite having some very innovative and extensive workplace bullying legislation in Norway, a case can still take 8 years to reach their Supreme Court.

There are many paradoxes in the laws covering workplace bullying. For example, in some jurisdictions[30] you are required to immediately inform your employer about the impact of the bullying on you, even though it may escalate the bullying. If you challenge your employer, he may retaliate by manipulating evidence to prove your incompetence. Some jurisdictions expect proof of the bully's intention to harm, although you can be injured regardless of intent, while others need proof that the bullying occurred. Many jurisdictions disregard trauma symptoms, especially those specifically demonstrated by victims of workplace bullying. Victims are sometimes forced to wait years for the validating, though meagre, compensation until their condition has stabilised, yet they need this finalising legal process to move on.

It is vital that you understand your local legal options, the processes involved, the hazards in obtaining them and any lack of public justice attached to gagging clauses. Currently, full justice for victims of workplace bullying is never possible in most jurisdictions because they are not validated immediately at work. However, legal action may provide some acknowledgment, resolution and closure.

Dealing with lawyers

'My attorney's opening argument was as follows: "Your Honor, I know you handle many workers compensation cases where an employee who works with defective machinery is injured, and they're awarded workers compensation benefits. In our case I will prove that Mr Smith's injury was caused by a defective manager with a defective management style." The judge immediately sat up and paid attention!'

You will require an appropriate lawyer for each jurisdiction you select when pursing a legal remedy for workplace bullying. Your lawyer also needs to be competent in the specific area of law you require and have a good reputation with targets. He or she needs to be respectful, return your messages and provide clear time frames. Since you know your employer better than they do, it is your responsibility to provide your lawyer with as much evidence as possible. When choosing a lawyer there are a number of things you need to keep in mind:

- Shop around for a lawyer who specialises in bullying, harassment, human rights, injury or employment issues.
- Consult your union's lawyers, the local law institute, internet lists, free community legal centres, lawyers who offer brief free legal advice, provide pro bono or work on a 'no win, no fee' basis.
- Obtain a clear financial picture about expected costs from your lawyer, including what you pay for, what your company or union pay for and the costs the lawyer will cover if you lose.
- Compare the consequences and advantages of using expert, expensive lawyers who know what to do, compared to using a nonexpert lawyer. If you cannot afford a lawyer, find a legal advocate or do it yourself with extensive research and advice from those with prior experience.
- Beware of using a lawyer in a small town who operates solely within their strong old boys' networks.

- Legal costs are generally very high; do not mortgage your home or use your superannuation in the faulty pursuit of justice, which like a gambling machine, is usually programmed for you to lose!

The legal jungle

'I felt so humiliated by the whole experience I didn't want anyone to witness my "shame". At my workers compensation hearing I chose not have anyone in the room to support me. My three main support people were witnesses and wouldn't sit in court until their evidence was heard. I now realise that this was a mistake. I must have appeared to the magistrate like a pathetic human being. Judicial officers of the court need to see that others support and agree with your view of the situation. They may feel more accountable if they know the general public is taking an interest in the proceedings, as well as their judgment, which may then come under scrutiny by others.'

Perhaps it is the biblical tradition of an eye for an eye, or the fantasy solutions found in television courtroom dramas. For whatever reason, many people seek their day in court, whether for compensation and justice, to punish their former bully and employer, or to stop others from bullying. Although you may feel partially validated by standing up in a court, you can risk further traumatisation. Legal success is like finding a needle in a haystack and you may be shocked at the lack of justice you encounter. Most legal systems require eyewitnesses, who may be too scared because they will be targeted next. Many legal outcomes yield unsatisfying results, such as resignations, real or false redundancies, or early retirement. Financial payouts never provide adequate compensation for your injuries, loss of earning capacity, and most likely, the loss of a job you loved. Currently, it is highly unlikely that any financial compensation is higher than what you would have earned at work had you not been injured. Even high-profile victims with millions of dollars in compensation payouts, wish they had never been bullied out of their job and can find it hard to move on.

Most male solicitors, barristers and judges are oblivious to female bullying because unlike a workplace accident such as falling on a slippery floor and breaking a leg, the bullying is subtle and unseen by witnesses, but nevertheless devastating. This will make them blind to the injuries caused by workplace bullying. Instead, they only want proof that the bullying occurred, even though you can be injured when there is no proof. A legal contest is often not based on what is right or wrong, but about who can fight tougher, longer and smarter.

What's a day in court worth?

> During cross-examination the defence barrister challenged the witness, 'Someone's told you what I'm going to be asking'. 'Yeah', the witness replied. The barrister asked who. The witness pointed to the prosecutor. Then the barrister made the mistake of asking a question for which he did not already know the answer, 'What did he tell you?' 'He said you're a bully, a dickhead and you mess with people's minds,' the witness replied.

> The lawyer said that this woman had a really good case and did everything he could for her. 'I am disgusted. She won the case but she didn't really win because the tribunal didn't give her costs so what she was awarded got eaten by her costs.'

Large, adversarial organisations can afford the best and most expensive legal advice to delay and procrastinate any legal claim. They can exhaust your energies and drain your financial resources so you stop fighting and give up before you obtain justice. Once you go to court their bully barristers will fight you at every point. They will pick on minor details, such as gaps in your memory, to undermine your testimony and make you appear an unreliable witness, or challenge paralysed victims as to why they did not report events earlier. They attempt to discredit expert witnesses by picking on little details, such as the contents of a report or their qualifications, to avoid investigating your injury. You can win a case but lose on appeal. Bullies may countersue in retaliation, win on appeal and intimidate their own legal departments.

Ultimately, your legal and human rights depend on what you can fight for within your industry, with the support of your union, perseverance, family situation, financial support structures, an accurate medico–legal assessment, the adequacy of the law and your lawyers. Regardless of this long, painful process, by giving a testimony, receiving compensation, making their employer accountable, and highlighting the evils of bullying, many people do feel validated and find some closure to move on.

Before you seek your day in court, work out what you hope to achieve and whether the risks are worth the pain and effort. Apart from the high risk of losing, because insurance companies dread a flood of claims, they also include high legal fees, time involved, your physical and psychological health, relationships with family and friends, career, professional reputation and financial future. In addition, some organisations settle on the steps just before you go into court to avoid publicity. They force you to sign confidentiality agreements that take away your right to speak publicly and therefore validate your experiences.

Thus, work out how far you are prepared to take your case when it creates a long delay in rebuilding your life after the bullying. Review the timeframe for every court action; for example, applying for workers compensation, or suing for unfair dismissal. Calculate other risks or advantages of legal proceedings such as complex legal issues, the jargon and courtroom games, losing on appeal, and the impact on your health, career and family.

Don't feel compelled to go to court because someone else wants justice. Find out what happened in similar cases and discuss your options with those who have been through a similar legal process. Make sure that your support network can handle your stress, and obtain quality psychological support. Assess your witnesses' loyalty and their ability to handle the legal battlefield. Consider the impact on your life of signing confidentiality clauses.

Ultimately, your best advice is to prepare for the worst and hope for the best. Remember though that legal action takes months or even years to be resolved. Most targets need validation and a quick resolution to get on with their life. Any lawsuit is the last resort. Try to find the best options, do as much as you can, emotionally and financially. Then identify when you need to say, '*Enough is enough, I did what I could*' and move on and begin your new life.

CHAPTER ELEVEN

Action for organisations

❝John worked for a small company. He enjoyed the work, but hated the exclusion, bitching, rumours and 'cherrypickers' (staff who took projects they liked or left them incomplete). Some employees appeared to be protected. Eventually, he made a formal complaint.

The CEO invited me to spend a session to discuss bullying at John's workplace and help create a common language. The following week I interviewed each employee. Everyone, including those who hadn't thought a session on workplace bullying was warranted, had been affected. Not only was John correct about the extent of the bullying, in addition, performance and productivity for the whole workplace was reduced. Targets, bullies and witnesses had symptoms — for example, tears, nausea, sleep difficulties, poor concentration, alcohol use and weight gain. Afterwards, everyone collaborated in focused discussions about how to restructure the company to create a fairer, safer and productive culture; there was no blame, shame or legal threat.

Later, I sat down with the CEO and discussed our approach. Had he asked for an investigation and mediation, he would have missed out on essential factors, such as the incompetent bully who was also feeling bullied, or the head office bully who initiated and influenced bullying in this branch. In other words, he could have 'pulled out the weeds but left the nasty roots behind'. ❞

Respect and resilience

Most organisations want to remain in business, expand if possible and stay profitable. They don't want to waste or lose money. Although any business is controlled by the economic bottom line, when employees are not feeling safe or respected, they cannot work effectively because their attitudes and values influence their level of work satisfaction and job performance.

Basically, employees who experience constructive working relationships within an open learning culture will be more motivated than those shredded by conflict and backstabbing.

Thus, like a family, school or sports club, the workplace is a system. It requires clear structures to function effectively, and appropriate social skills to work together. A best practice organisation creates a cooperative, collaborative work culture where employees feel safe, involved and empowered. This requires strong leadership and effective management to promote clear goals and values.

Therefore, companies need to review their business ethics, and incorporate ideas such as social responsibility and social and human capital to reinforce the concept of valuing staff. Clearly, it is better business practice to respect every employee and treat them as a valuable asset, instead of fostering gladiatorial survival games.

Organisations need to structure their work culture — both how managers organise employees to work within their social climate and how employees view their organisation. The work culture predicts the company's success; thus organisations who manage people well outperform those who do not by 30 to 40%. There is no place for bullies in a well-run organisation.[1] Thus building strong interpersonal skills at all levels is fundamental for the healthy workplace.

However, even in the best company, creative or critical conflict will occur. Life is not always that easy; work is not a picnic, and employees need the skills to handle difficult people and feel comfortable to confront, challenge and dispute differences, not avoid them. These differences need to be managed so that the organisation benefits from creative conflicts and resolves critical conflicts. Thus there are many reasons for an employer to stop bullying behaviours. These include health and safety, financial costs, reducing incompetence and fraud, as well as improving leadership, work culture, performance and social responsibility. Consequently, every company needs effective procedures for dealing with disputes, conflict and bullying behaviours.

Change

Following the deaths of several aggressive male baboons in a troop being studied in Kenya by scientists, it was observed that the restructured troop became more peaceful and affectionate.

There was less fighting and bullying. The biologist Robert Sapolsky from Stanford University said that new males learn that 'It pays to be nice' and 'We don't do things like that around here'. If wild baboons can modify their behaviours, then there's hope for the workplace![2]

Change is an integral part of business life. Employees are constantly adapting to changes, such as the extra pressure of Christmas stocktake sales, emergencies and pursuing bonuses. More recently, in countries where smoking inside has been outlawed, employees have had to adapt to taking short breaks outside to smoke. When employees change their attitude, they modify their behaviours and adapt to change, and then the organisational norms, culture and climate can improve. Clearly, altering the work climate and culture to value all employees is a sensible goal. Although change takes time, organisational psychologists can usually achieve some effective change within a year.

Organisations need to assume responsibility when there is bullying, as it signifies systemic dysfunction. This involves changing their values from condoning predatory, adversarial cultures to empowering collaborative, competent workplaces. Although some organisations must acknowledge legal liability, and others employ every trick to deny it, they need to validate employees' perceptions and take responsibility for resolving disputes. The actual cost of management training, focus groups, intervention programs, counselling, and prevention strategies seems insignificant in comparison to the damages associated with bullying. It is usually cheaper to retain and retrain employees than to eliminate them. Aside from professional support and training costs, it is inexpensive to rebalance the power relationship between the target, bully and witnesses, especially if intervention takes place early on. Ultimately it is financially and ethically more profitable for companies to acknowledge and reduce bullying than foster, deny or condone it.

Leadership skills

'The onus should be upon the entire organisation to make sure the policy is working. Although board members don't interact with staff, they can't hide behind the policy. They require appropriate strategies to obtain the correct perspective and good corporate governance. Then the manager should detect the early warning signs instead of relying on the policy because a

victim may be unable to utilise formal avenues. In my case, I just thought I was doing everything wrong and failing to correct it no matter how hard I tried.'

Lions are pretty tough animals; however, they follow their leader because they generally find more food if they hunt together. The chief executive officer's role is to build organisational resilience and improve productivity; in other words, to engage and influence employees towards goals endorsed by the leader. The responsible chief needs to mentor the psychological health of his organisation because healthy, happy employees are more productive. He can reinforce this message and monitor its progress throughout the company via his managers. Like the ecosystem of a rainforest, the CEO can establish a cohesive, self-supporting unit that works together. When he listens and engages, shows respect, sets reasonable boundaries, and gives and receives constructive feedback, he provides a role model that can act as a template for managers to establish effective teams within small groups or at senior management level. Consequently, the CEO needs to be task- and people-orientated and know what is occurring at the grassroots level and middle management level, as these managers may feel pressured to portray a productive, cohesive picture when it is not.

Good management isn't rocket science!

When Motorola, a software engineering group, began regular monthly meetings to acknowledge accomplishments, it saw patent applications increase, work problems resolved more quickly and a renewed sense of team spirit and unity.[3]

Managers who think outside the square know that production and efficiency are improved when they get their staff to rally behind them. This can only happen when they give respect and empathy to every employee and train everyone to employ empathy with every colleague. The fact is that no-one rallies behind someone they dislike. Good managers encourage a culture of honesty, humour, integrity, trust, openness and inclusion. They listen carefully to their staff and use their feedback. They collaborate with their staff, encourage them to become more effective by rewarding and promoting those with good people skills and empowering each person to try their best. They regard change as a challenging part of business. The only area in which a manager is expected to be better than his staff is in his talent as a leader!

Managers need to understand the value of a bully-free workplace and realise that when employees feel safe, they achieve more. Effective communication skills create a work synergy leading to fewer errors, improved skills, efficient systems, improved motivation and improved client relations and so forth. Although managers should value every employee, they need to understand that the collective output exceeds any individual's output, thus by building a collaborative team they can successfully confront workplace stressors such as change, restructuring or personality differences. A good manager can't afford the costs associated with condoning bullying at his workplace.

Good managers take pride in employing effective, assertive leadership skills. They use their emotional and social intelligence to identify and monitor any personal and interpersonal difficulties at work, to regulate their own behaviours and manage those of others, especially those who are vulnerable. Their role model is a template for their staff. They lead through their relationships and flexible manner rather than through tangible rewards. They require training in problem-solving, communication and conflict resolution skills, as well as regular monitoring to develop and adapt these skills.

The effective manager

To effectively manage people it is important not to confuse management with bullying. It is not necessary to adopt a 'bullish' attitude to staff in order for instructions to be understood.

Although bullying is less likely to occur in safe, friendly environments, it *can* occur, just like weeds in a garden and cobwebs in your home that spring up despite regular cleaning. The effective manager realises that stopping bullying is good for business and that he needs to confront any bullying before it escalates out of control. The effective manager accepts responsibility for creating a fair go for all culture. He values every employee, validates their concerns, and mentors and monitors them.

The effective manager provides positive and constructive feedback to employees to help them improve their work performance. He intervenes and adjusts inappropriate behaviours, including his own, without becoming aggressive or passive. His leadership style reduces defensive behaviours, facilitates communication, lowers personal injury and reduces payback and corruption. When the effective manager removes bullying and improves staff performance, he understands that he automatically improves his status and power. Effective managers follow the practices listed here to ensure a productive workplace. They will:

- understand the difference between conflict, bullying and violence
- distinguish between genuine or malicious complaints
- identify manipulative metaphors — for example, 'Women overreact' or 'That's John'
- look for mobbing by the 'boys' club' or 'girls' clique'
- identify abrasive managers
- search beyond the facade for hidden agendas, such as oversensitive targets and underperforming bullies
- confront issues instead of dividing, rejecting or alienating staff
- separate performance and disciplinary issues from bullying
- create a structure for occupational justice and the respectful resolution of conflict
- implement disciplinary guidelines when necessary.

A safety kit to safeguard staff

Leaders should listen and listen and listen. Only through listening can they find out what's really going on. If someone comes in to raise an issue with the leader and the leader does not allow the individual to state their case fully and to get emotions out in the open, the leader is likely to understand only a piece of the story and the problem probably will not be solved.[4]

The above quote from the report by the Accident Investigation Board into the Columbia space shuttle re-entry disaster in 2003 reveals incidents from the testimonies of quality assurance inspectors who were manipulated to accept work that had been originally refused. Thus NASA's organisational culture and the pattern of breakdowns cost the lives of seven astronauts!

There are several strategies an organisation can set in place to help provide a safety kit to safeguard its employees:

- *The buck stops here* — The CEO and board are responsible for every systemic layer of the organisational hierarchy, including managers, line managers, contact officers and HR departments. They need to ensure bullying is stopped, and help every employee feel safe.

- *Commitment* — Managers need regular and unscheduled departmental audits to ascertain that procedures are effective and to enforce their ethical values and legal obligations.

- *Vigilance* — Look for the little things that go wrong because then you will not miss the big ones; for example, unhappy faces, tears and angry outbursts, absenteeism, increased staff turnover.

- *Compassion* — Value every employee by providing respect, acknowledgment, confidentiality and care.

- *Identify the core issue* — Employers need to understand that the escalating conflict is the core issue, not the target or bully. They need to resolve the conflict with all involved and prevent targets turning into bullies and bullies into targets.[5]
- *Deal with it immediately* — All that targets require is acknowledgment or validation and a safe workplace. Managers need to train their staff to provide immediate localised support and take reconciliatory action to end the dispute. This is more respectful, cost-effective and reduces the likelihood of any conflict escalating.
- *Develop a consistent approach* — Organisations need consistency across all departments, levels and associated companies. If bullying occurs in one section then it needs to be audited everywhere else.
- *Collaborate* — Employers need to create ethical liaisons to work together within their organisation and with external agencies to help targets and bullies, such as working with insurance companies, health professionals, lawyers and rehabilitation providers.
- *Use the correct tools* — Many organisations use the bulldozer approach to resolve a bullying incident when pliers would be more effective and less inflammatory, and so need to identify when a simple direct approach will suffice or when a complex investigation is warranted.
- *Beware false allegations* — In addition to the common misuse of the word *bullying*, behaviours can be misinterpreted or exaggerated; thus targets and bullies can be wrongly labelled and mistreated.
- *Remember your legal obligations* — The law may seem invisible or ineffective at times but employers may be made financially accountable for bullying. CEOs, company directors, employers, managers and bullies may be sued and fined (and even jailed in countries like France).
- *Multiple approaches are the answer* — 'It was not one single ingenious thing that made the difference, but the sum of many small moves'.[6] Research shows that school bullying is reduced when a variety of techniques are used. Thus it is impossible to rely upon any single methodology in the workplace to resolve all systemic difficulties.

Strategies for organisations to reduce bullying behaviours

Debbie worked for a prestigious stockbroking company that prided itself on its zero tolerance bullying policies. At first she ignored the bully's references to her appearance, sex life and professional competence, but finally she went to Judy, head of HR, and made an unofficial complaint.

Judy met the man and asked for his version. He admitted to some comments, while minimising and denying others. However, Judy had interviewed other witnesses and had sufficient evidence. She reminded him of their policy and pointed out the consequences for bullying behaviours, and referred to his past record, which showed earlier bullying incidents. She provided some options and a warning to change, otherwise his employment would be terminated. The company paid for his psychology consultations.

There are many different theories and practices to develop psychologically healthy, best practice, productive workplaces. Some reduce the likelihood of bullying by improving the general culture and climate (without referring to bullying), others develop specific polices and structures to reduce bullying.

The following suggestions are based on the author's experience with educational institutions and organisations. However, there are countless ways to reduce bullying and you can integrate these steps into your policies, practices and programs. There is no clear path to take, you can mix and match as long as your goals are clear and you achieve them.

Step 1: Implement company values, policies, codes of conduct

Annette, a senior manager, believes that if her bosses were compelled to sign a code of conduct, she could have confronted them and obtained justice.

A company policy demonstrates how your organisation regards employee relationships and should give a clear and consistent message about harassment and bullying.[7] It reflects the core values and expectations of how employees should work within the company culture. Both the code and policies need to be respected, implemented and maintained to create a structural and cultural change, as well as a fair workplace. Organisations that respect and implement their policies may also be in a better legal position if taken to court.

The code of conduct should be more comprehensive than the policy and, like other restrictions (e.g., for fraud and harassment), specify the major categories of bullying behaviours. The employer, managers, union and staff must be involved in the design of codes, policies and programs to ensure their success. The code and policy should represent their requirements and not be cloned from elsewhere. It should:

- identify the major bullying behaviours, explain individual and systemic damage, the fair management and resolution of bullying and its consequences
- clarify what will or will not be tolerated
- be comprehensive and based upon law
- be reflected in mission statements (e.g., *Value and respect everyone*; *Inclusion not isolation*) but, more importantly, by what it does
- be provided to all and expressed simply in plain English and other languages spoken in the workplace
- if possible be included in everyone's employment contract
- in any case, be included on the standard business behaviour guideline that every employee should sign annually.

Step 2: Adopt preventative practices

> I recommend the 'green, yellow and red light' program. People say 'yellow light' as a warning if they're unhappy with someone's behaviour and red involves reporting. In one company it reduced complaints from 70 to 10 complaints.[8]

Organisations need to reduce the likelihood of bullying ever occurring and reduce the damage when it does. They require unity without uniformity. They need to improve working conditions, such as clearly defining role descriptions, improving the work culture and climate, showing their respect towards staff (e.g., empathy, equal opportunity, family friendly work–life balance) and incorporating prevention policies and practices to reduce the likelihood of bullying occurring.

Improving professional standards

Improving day-to-day professional standards is a good way to begin preventing workplace bullying. Standards can be improved by:

- implementing effective job design for all staff and then clearly defining and publicising every job description and each employee's roles and responsibilities

- ensuring every employee has sufficient induction, training, regular mentoring, and material resources for their job requirements
- respecting fair and equitable work requirements
- supervising all new staff, including managers, for a period of time to help them settle into an approach to team work
- monitoring managers' management skills regularly
- assigning work/rosters fairly according to experience and competence (not power or politics)
- understanding that yelling, swearing, and thumping tables do not belong in the modern workplace, nor does micromanaging, exploitation, or public humiliation
- training managers in how to instruct, delegate, mentor, listen, show empathy and use feedback to improve their work relationships and thereby improve productivity and their professional status
- conducting regular performance appraisals in conjunction with a review of the employee's interpersonal skills and recording any situations where they reduced bullying incidents appropriately
- preventing misuse or misunderstanding of nepotism — clarify, justify, but don't deny — including cliques/clubs, friends, family, union members
- avoiding role fossilisation where employees make decisions based solely on their past experiences without being based in reality or showing respect for others
- assessing the labour and materials required for each project/task to ensure there are adequate staffing levels, materials and equipment where possible
- reviewing and comparing each exit interview to each employee's work history.

Changing the cultural climate

Likewise an organisation's cultural climate needs to be carefully nurtured to prevent the development of bully-friendly practices. Changes to the cultural climate can include:

- teaching courtesy, work conduct and manners; for example, greet known staff and show friendly interest in colleagues

- conducting regular staff meetings, preferably weekly, but at a minimum every month, to debrief, improve relationships, and discuss professional and interpersonal concerns

- providing training in assertiveness, conflict resolution and communication skills to help employees with interpersonal difficulties

- empowering staff by providing opportunities for feedback at forums, focus groups, brainstorming sessions, graffiti boards, blogs, and so forth

- developing effective, well-functioning real or virtual work groups by rewarding teamwork, so that employees adjust to one another, work together and share the trust required to resolve differences

- collaborating with employees to improve the work environment, including good lighting and ventilation, ergonomically sound equipment — like chairs, tables and headsets — as well as extras such as music, fresh paint, plants or personal mementos

- helping employees feel safe and comfortable; for example, reducing isolation and using structured surveillance such as closed circuit televisions, especially in isolated areas and basements

- providing safe work and social functions, using clear guidelines for behaviour, including restricting alcohol consumption and ensuring a range of drinks and food is provided.

Preventing bullying

Specific practices to prevent bullying must also be built into an organisation's regular functions. These practices include:

- collaborating with employee representatives (from as many divisions or areas as possible), unions and professional associations to develop programs for safer workplaces

- training HR staff to understand bullying, how it should be investigated, and how to intervene with collaborative restorative solutions

- changing the work culture to accept and integrate people who are different; for example, older employees, those from other cultural backgrounds, homosexuals and women

- developing an early grassroots warning system by appointing trained contact people to handle bullying complaints

- training internal workplace mediators with the power to intervene and resolve disputes

- protecting whistleblowers so that employees can report formally and informally, such as through anonymous helplines or an employee suggestion box

- implementing the laws of natural justice for all employees

- teaching managers to transfer or retrain ineffective employees

- including antibullying behaviours in workplace agreements

- ensuring visual images such as prints or posters on walls are not offensive

- never confronting an employee of the opposite gender alone in a closed office.

Ensuring cyber safety

In today's workplace the use and abuse of computers needs to be governed by explicit procedures. These could include:

- using social networking as a tool for extending relationships within the workplace

- describing, reinforcing and regularly reviewing safe, ethical, economic cyber usage (including computers and phones)

- using signed contracts for 'netiquette' to prevent difficulties occurring

- where possible, encouraging employees to communicate and resolve difficulties face-to-face rather than electronically

- monitoring all computer and phone usage to stop abusive, unproductive and inefficient communication, and reducing misuse of internet sites such as MySpace, Facebook, Twitter, LinkedIn and cyber games, internet shopping and phone texting

- warning staff that they are liable for inappropriate cyber use, which is criminal in some states or countries

- warning staff that all their electronic communications are not private and may be read by the information technology section of the company and their manager at any stage.

Breaking down barriers

It is important that there are open channels of communication within a workplace. Organisations can improve this process by remaining barriers through:

- providing safe channels for employees to communicate regularly with senior management, such as via email, focus groups, regular meetings, or short meetings
- creating comfortable open workspaces, like a village square
- emphasising teamwork instead of hierarchy, such as different titles where the 'supervisor' becomes a 'coordinator'
- providing everyone with identical discounts, artwork, coffee, childcare, and parking rights
- creating social opportunities to break down barriers through pleasurable activities, such as a gardening club, gym or walking group
- encouraging bottom-up communication or reverse mentoring; for example, enable young graduates to educate senior executives in cyber usage and social networking.

Involving workmates and witnesses

Workmates become effective change agents when there is an active witness support system or buddy structure within their workplace. Employees need training to identify bullying, support targets or confront bullies without threatening or being threatened themselves and targeted next. They also need support, protection and encouragement (perhaps a reward) to report to management, otherwise they can also be injured and leave.

Creating a village culture

The Australian concept of mateship is a good system of social survival. It grew out of the trenches of wartime and the pioneering hardships of settling a new land. It is reinforced every time there is a communal tragedy, such as bushfires. Just like the American 'buddy', English 'chum' or French 'ami', mateship means that we stick together like mortar in times of stress.

The socially responsible organisation encourages workplace friendships to maintain a shared culture and productive workplace. Just like living in a village, everyone should be accepted, tolerated, included, treated fairly and supported.

Step 3: Maintain a bully blocking taskforce

> *Joe realised that he should have reported the bullying incidents 9 months earlier, but he didn't know where to go to for advice or help.*

Dealing with workplace bullying is such a major challenge for any company it cannot be left to one person. Organisations need to appoint a committee to develop responsible programs or delegate the work to an existing one, so that everyone feels involved and represented. This task-force needs representatives from employees, unions and management; and links with HR staff, occupational health and safety representatives and employee assistance providers. They need the power and resources to conduct research, develop policy and procedures, and implement, monitor and regularly evaluate safe work practices, such as exploring with targets how the workplace can be improved. They may involve independent experts such as organisational psychologists or lawyers to assist with prevention, training, crisis intervention, counselling and rehabilitation.

Step 4: Assess the bullying

> *Despite the fact that there've been serious complaints of bullying over a number of years and numerous staff leaving, Terry's employer denied bullying. He described it as a 'personality problem' and did nothing.*

Bullying can occur anywhere at work. However, bullying cultures create smokescreens and many managers have blind spots. Thus many targets find it difficult to describe subtle, sustained toxic behaviours. Some employees leave without complaining, others complain when it is too late for simple remedies. Assessing workplace bullying can be akin to estimating the size of an iceberg. You might identify the targets with their presenting symptoms, or the psychopathic bully, but not the underlying systemic causes or damage. You need to ask what is going wrong, not who is wrong.

At some stage you may need to compare the target's perception and symptoms to objective evidence, applying a similar assessment to the bully, as well as assessing the performance and productivity of everyone else involved, especially any mobs/cliques/clubs. Regardless of whether or not an employee has contributed to the interpersonal crisis, you need to assess whether anyone else in their position would feel bullied. You need regular, comprehensive audits to identify bullying.

Audit objectives:

- Who does what, to whom, where, why, when?
- What is the personal, interpersonal and financial impact upon the target, bully, onlookers and organisation?
- To what extent does the bullying indicate organisational problems?
- What successful strategies can be instigated to enable individuals and the organisation to reduce bullying?
- What are the ineffective strategies?

Assessment options:

- information/training sessions
- interest/focus groups
- performance reviews (feedback without fear of retaliation)
- valid, confidential questionnaires[9]
- organisational effectiveness, welfare or employee opinion surveys that include bullying behaviours
- telephone/email helpline
- anonymous suggestion boxes
- video cameras
- confidential mentor systems
- consultative committees
- the '360-degree' approach.

Other sources of information:

- work-related injuries
- complaints — from employees or the public
- absenteeism figures
- disciplinary actions

- past employment history
- audits of computer usage and internet use (including user details, time, date, sites visited, length of time viewed and the computer or device used)
- risk-assessment procedures
- exit interviews, immediately and 6 months later (when the employee's fear is lowered)
- contact with the target or the bully's previous referees when difficulties arise.

Step 5: Maintain adequate records

> 'Despite years of good performance reviews they listened to the new manager and blamed me just after I complained about the bullying.'

Organisations need to maintain up-to-date, comprehensive records on every employee, to monitor their employment history and note if or when employees take legal action. This includes performance reviews, disciplinary action, personal injuries and any interventions. Records need to establish a comprehensive work history so that incompetent managers do not change their mind suddenly, sabotage an employee with an excellent work performance history or jeopardise their company's productivity and legal position. If there is bullying, record the initial complaint, investigation processes, interviews, actions, sanctions and follow-ups. You need to compare and cross-reference the bully's history with their target's history, include those of onlookers (e.g., via exit interviews).

Step 6: Harness public relations

> Staff need to know that bullying and harassment won't be tolerated, that people who use bullying behaviours must change them and if you're experiencing bullying, initiate action through your organisation.[10]

The key to a safe system is communication, because abuse and violence survive when condoned. The secret of dealing with bullying is *don't keep it secret!* Although bullying is an unpopular word, it cannot be totally camouflaged. People who describe bullying behaviours as *fun*, *horseplay* or *getting the job done* need to know that it is abusive and unproductive.

An organisation demonstrates its commitment to reducing bullying by promoting antibullying messages and demonstrating how everyone benefits from reducing it. Apart from consequences, it is the simplest way to develop awareness and change attitudes. It is practical to utilise official and unofficial lines of communication (e.g., *word of mouth* or *local grapevine*) to provide the key messages.

Written information needs to be expressed simply, in all relevant languages. Explain all major terms clearly so that they are used appropriately, and reduce false or inaccurate reporting; for example, 'diversity', 'discrimination', 'mobbing', 'harassment', as well as 'performance review' and 'disciplinary actions'.

An organisation's own public relations machinery can be used to demonstrate how the system operates, for example, via case studies.

Antibullying slogans might include: *Stop bullying, it's good for business. Bullying is a workplace hazard. Bullying is a work cancer. We care about staff.* Promotional aids might include staff manuals, wallet-size mission statements, payslip tips, posters, solid or electronic noticeboards, intranet, newsletters, email, or text messages.

Step 7: Promote information, training and skills

> Hank used rough and tough behaviour to walk over people on his climb to the top of the corporate ladder. Although he enjoyed using the 'F' word, staff found it threatening. The HR department forced him to listen to complaints and alter his behaviours. His psychologist suggested he wear a comfortable rubber band around his wrist, and each time he swore he was instructed to pull hard. He learned very quickly that swearing equals pain! Since then he's collaborating with his team and getting better results.

Most bullying occurs because many people do not understand and actually realise what they are doing, or do not know a better way to relate and confront difficulties. They change very quickly, however, when they view their behaviours on a television screen!

Training ensures that everyone understands what workplace bullying involves and the damage it causes, and reinforces the message that it will not be tolerated. It empowers employees to relate respectfully and resolve differences without abusing one another. It creates opportunities and skills for employees to work out fair solutions. Training enables managers, HR staff, targets, onlookers and bullies to work together. It reduces the likelihood of further bullying occurring by changing beliefs and behaviours. Ultimately, staff training reflects the organisation's commitment to reduce bullying.

Workplace bullying training programs need to take note of the following issues:

- Programs need to be regular and comprehensive, and not just designed to reduce claims and other risks. Every employee — including the CEO, board members, senior management, supervisors, managers, part-time and contract staff — requires training.

- A program can be specific (to deal with workplace bullying) or integrated into general training (to improve productivity), but must always be identified as managing workplace bullying.

- Ideally, training should be linked to employment contracts, induction programs and performance reviews, so everyone attends and participates with respect.

- Programs should assist targets who move to a new job and require counselling to deal with their past bullying experiences, or coach them in how to block future bullying.

- Organisations can use internal staff and external experts, such as management consultants, lawyers or organisational psychologists, to conduct and run programs.

- Presentations need to be empowering, entertaining and nonthreatening as participants will not share, disclose or learn when threatened.

- Practical learning techniques should be used to transfer theory to the workplace; these include case discussions, role-plays (which demonstrate different bullying scenarios and respectful resolutions), hypotheticals, debates, films, DVDs, e-Learning (cost-effective but cannot replace face-to-face training) and virtual world training. Communication and conflict resolution skills always require face-to-face training and practice.

- Different times and locations — such as full-day workshops, seminars, conferences — should be used.

- The content of the programs should:
  - understand workplace bullying — description, causes, damage, injuries, costs, legal issues, the value of a bully-free culture and constructive solutions

- build emotional and social intelligence at work to train employees to identify anger and stress within themselves and others as well as respond with understanding; it should also encourage them to behave assertively, not aggressively or passively
- teach awareness by allowing employees to share past bullying experiences because most people have been bullied or have bullied others
- deal with any traumatic bullying experiences
- train staff in communication skills such as active listening, rapport-building, assertive language, negotiation skills, and dealing with difficult people
- teach managers how to value and mentor their staff and promote effective, collaborative team skills to improve work morale and productivity
- train employees to value constructive feedback; this improves performance and reduces incompetence.

Step 8: Use face-to-face interventions

> *The moment Bill got his new Blackberry the complaints began; people said his messages were short and mean. The HR department advised him to send courteous emails, not missiles.*

A good manager, like a racehorse trainer, needs to monitor his team regularly to identify warning signs of distress, such as unhappy facial expressions, tears, social exclusion, stress and angry outbursts. The simplest way to deal with bullying is to intervene immediately and encourage stressed staff to obtain help. You can use effective communication skills to create a safe working relationship — for example, via appropriate eye contact, non-threatening body language and careful listening skills. Make sure you obtain all evidence from each person's perspective, including the target, bully and bystanders, as well as any professionals that are involved such as doctors and psychologists.

The first simple step of face-to-face intervention is asking questions. Courteous questioning may be enough to show your team that you will not allow further bullying. Questioning should follow these basic themes listed here.

Clarify

- *Could you repeat what you just said?*
- *Do you realise what you've done?*
- *This is awful. What else is going on here?*

- *I need to talk to you about what happened today.*
- *You sounded very angry, what's happening?*
- *You've lost your third secretary in 23 months. Each one had excellent references and mentioned your bullying behaviours in their exit interviews. What help do you need to change?*
- *I hear that you exclude, demean and harass some staff. We need teamwork, so can you stop this on your own or do you need mentoring?*

Confront
- *I find this really offensive.*
- *This is awful, I'm shocked to hear this.*
- *I am concerned about X (the target).*
- *Bob says you give him too much work, while others do less. What's happening?*
- *Do you realise that Maggie is very upset at the way you treat her? She's taken two weeks off to recover.*
- *I'd like to discuss a certain matter with you, can we do it now or later?*
- *I won't listen to unfounded allegations.*
- *If you don't give Jack fair shifts you'll face consequences.*
- *Maria is extremely upset about your texts and emails. She wants to take legal action. What can you do to repair the hurt and damage?*

Make constructive suggestions
- *Are you aware that your behaviours are banned in our company code?*
- *Angry people get heart attacks, try the calm approach.*
- *Jenny's upset that you don't send her some emails. Can you apologise for the oversight and send everybody the relevant emails?*
- *You speak nicely to clients and young Fred, the CEO's son, but I've heard that you abuse and criticise junior staff. They're upset and working less. Can you try and treat them like our clients or Fred?*
- *There's been an expensive turnover in young chefs (surgeons, teachers, and so on). What can you do to help them stay?*
- *I'm concerned about X (the target). What can we do to help him feel less stressed?*

When you receive a bullying complaint don't condone, condemn or collude, but consider each person's perspective. It can be difficult to distinguish between a target, provocative person or bully, and some people are oblivious to their mean behaviours or mirror their stressful work climate. Complaints need to be taken seriously, investigated and appropriate action taken. Your aim is to create a win–win situation for everyone. You need to review your own role model. Staff copy what you do, not what you say. Remember when asked to intervene in a bullying dispute to:

- investigate each person's perception and how they have been affected by the bullying
- separate evidence from personality (even difficult personalities can be correct)
- avoid confusing dissent or constructive feedback with disloyalty
- behave assertively and provide constructive feedback
- refrain from interrupting, demeaning or threatening, and avoid aggressive or abusive behaviours
- not show disrespect or destroy any employee's self-esteem, otherwise you could provoke them to sabotage or bully in a more subversive manner
- use flexibility in dealing with different or difficult personalities.

Helping powerless employees

Once a target reports a bullying experience, listen carefully to obtain their story, consider their prior history, understand their perception and validate their experience, even if the evidence does not fully support their claim. Apart from providing advice, help and support, find out what else the target wants changed (if possible) and refer them, when appropriate, for counselling, coaching or mentoring. Provide regular follow-ups to make sure that they are managing. Some suggestions on what to say to targets include:

- *I've heard that Jack's making jokes about you. How do you feel?*
- *You've changed lately. What's wrong?*
- *Why have you been away so much?*
- *When I give you a performance review, you're upset with my feedback. Is it my style, content or both that upset you?*

- *What can we do to reduce stress around here?*
- *How are you being treated unfairly?*
- *What would you like X to do differently?*
- *What can you do differently?*

Remember that some targets use personal or work difficulties to blame someone else. Investigate further, obtain professional advice and use a nonconfronting style to help them manage. Look out for former targets who superimpose their previous traumatic experiences onto the current job, thus exaggerating or exacerbating their perceptions.

Managing difficult bullies

> *Maria's family own a large manufacturing business and put up with a nasty, controlling bully for years. They paid him well because he was 'irreplaceable'. Meanwhile good employees weren't supported and left when he bullied them. Suddenly he left at a time when the company really needed him. They were forced to reassess their needs and employed someone quite different, who is cheaper and better, and everything's going smoothly! Now they regret the time it took for him to leave.*

Bullying flows down from the top like lava. Many bullies need to protect themselves from being bullied, or bully others because that is their survival role model. They do not understand the destructive nature of bullying upon themselves or their bullying behaviours on others. They survive and thrive by playing games, and deny their inappropriate behaviours. They regard confrontation as devastating, and can become defensive, or threaten or blame others. They can retaliate with subtler bullying, sue for wrongful dismissal or defamation, or use industrial action to sabotage their employer.

When dealing with a difficult bully make sure before initiating any formal procedures — such as an investigation, mediation or conciliation — that you try to resolve the conflict informally. First, obtain the facts from the target (where possible, respecting confidentiality issues), then discuss the matter with the alleged bully, asking them for their version of events. As well as researching the history of the alleged bully, other evidence should be considered, such as audiotapes, videos, performance reviews, sick leave statistics and relevant exit statements.

Check out if the alleged bully's conduct is fair or not. Is this behaviour an acceptable part of their job requirements or not? What is the impact of their behaviour on the workplace? Investigate the situation from the bully's perspective — are they unaware, under pressure or under attack?

Share your concern about the target's difficulties and ask the bully to understand and acknowledge the target's perception (as distinct from the evidence). Ask for their collaboration to resolve the dispute; for example, explain, reframe, apologise, performance manage the target appropriately, provide clear instructions. When confronting the bully, provide constructive, respectful feedback. Using assertive language, tell them what behaviours need to be changed and practised, such as empathy training, assertive communication skills (to express their frustration assertively instead of being aggressive or passive). Offer them professional assistance to modify their behaviours, such as counselling, coaching, mentoring, training. Use humour such as 'Hey, have you got your cranky pants on today?'

Make sure you do not bully them yourself or blame them without clear evidence. Keep an eye out for inconsistencies, contradictions, cover-ups (for incompetence) or lying; this means comparing what they say and how they say it with what you hear. Just like a customs official, closely observe contradictory eye messages, facial expressions, body language and gestures. Beware of manipulative games such as denial, blaming, excuses or superficial charm.

If the bully does not improve their behaviours, consequences need to be clearly expressed and implemented.

Step 9: Manage bullying incidents

> BHP Billiton employs thousands of people in many countries. The person operating their international telephone helpline listens to employee complaints, obtains facts and consults with others. He assists the target or bully, human resources or managers. He has power to report right up the hierarchy.
>
> Deal with it early, deal with if firmly and have it come from the top.[11]

There are three major types of crisis management: people crises, natural disasters and physical plant/technology incidents. Organisations have a duty of care towards their employees, whether it is exposure to toxic materials, faulty equipment or abusive people. Many organisations are prepared for critical incidents such as a fire or hold-up, but they also need procedures to deal with people incidents, such as conflict, violence and bullying. They cannot just blame targets for being vulnerable. In fact, in some countries, once the target warns their employer about their vulnerabilities, it may increase their employer's legal liability.

Intervention may be direct, such as resolving differences, or indirect and packaged, such as improving performance. The goal is to acknowledge the bullying and resolve the conflict, rather than prove a complaint. A flow chart of what will happen, when, how, by whom and how it could affect how when bullying is reported needs to be drawn up. The first contact for activation of the incident plan should be a trained, designated person, such as a supervisor, line manager, contact officer.[12] Ideally, this person has the power to intervene immediately, respect confidentiality and resolve the dispute. When choosing such people the following points should be considered:

- This person should be friendly, empathetic and supportive, with good communication and dispute resolution skills.
- They need to validate targets/bullies during this difficult period, and provide them with options while respecting other employees' perspectives.
- Targets can make an informal complaint to them or seek advice on other coping strategies.

The target/bully should also be able to consult a specialist within or outside the organisation for advice, options, support and action, including equal opportunity officers, a grievance person, HR staff, employment assistance personnel, occupational health and safety practitioners, doctors, or a lawyer or psychologist.

Step 10: Investigate complaints and resolve disputes

> *Sarah told her employer that five other women had witnessed the bullying. The company's investigator had skills in information technology, not investigations, and didn't even interview her witnesses!*

When a simple face-to-face discussion or informal approach fails or is not possible, then the process moves to a formal written complaint. Formal complaint procedures require an impartial investigation of the allegations and are designed to prove whether or not a complaint is substantiated. A formal bullying complaint should not be dismissed because there are no witnesses as the target may still have an injury, bystanders can be affected

and company performance lowered. Nor should the formal procedures rely on the biased evidence supplied by the bullies and their support team, which may include management. An effective investigation should:

- investigate the target's and alleged bully's past behaviours and employment history
- check if the alleged bully has a history of harassment
- ask whether the target was being unduly provocative or mobbed by the main group
- ask if the alleged bully and/or target have a diagnosable psychiatric disorder as assessed by a mental health professional
- not make any accusations of personality as a cause unless a psychiatrist/ psychologist has made a prior, clinical, evidence-based evaluation of an employee's personality and/or mental health problems(with their permission to release this confidential data)
- investigate the causes and symptoms of the target's injury; for example, the death of someone significant may cause psychological distress such as sadness, or a disorder such as depression, but it is different from the trauma caused by workplace bullying
- beware that when a target has experienced an earlier trauma, such as domestic violence or a car accident, they have a predisposition to becoming traumatised again — remember that workplace bullying trauma is a different injury

- collect witness statements and if key witnesses suddenly deny or alter their version, this may show that they are also being bullied and fear retribution.

Complaint interventions

There are many ways in which organisations can handle bullying complaints; these are listed in order of suitability.

Acknowledgement and restructuring

The most constructive approach is to bypass the *name, blame and shame* approaches. If complaints are made about bullying, investigate if bullying has occurred, by whom and how it has affected all employees and the company. As sustained bullying signifies a dysfunctional system, it requires restructuring.

- Provide employees with a solid seminar on what bullying involves and create a shared understanding and language.

- If possible, in a neutral location interview a selection of staff involved.

- Use a set list of interview questions to investigate employees' perceptions and experiences, without threatening anyone or sabotaging the evidence, such as, *What's been happening here? How did it affect you and others? What can be done to improve the working culture?*

- Obtain and record employees' suggestions to reduce bullying and improve the work culture.

- Consider other evidence, such as sick days, staff turnover, or inappropriate emails.

- Create a follow-up meeting to summarise findings.

- Acknowledge any generic bullying, personal injury or company damage.

- Organise discussion or focus groups to provide management with practical solutions. These can include building a fairer, safer and collaborative work culture via better staff supervision, regular meetings, positive reinforcement, implementing respectful behaviours, outlining consequences for inappropriate behaviours and organising some social or recreational activities.

- Establish follow-up sessions to monitor cultural improvements.

Restorative practices

Currently an effective, respectful method of dispute resolution is work-place conferencing, restorative practices or restorative justice (also known as conflict transformation or transformative justice.) It creates an impartial collaborative environment in which every person has equal power. Unlike mediation, where the imbalance of power remains static, this actually involves suspending hierarchy during the process.

This approach focuses upon what has happened, how people have been affected and what can be done to improve the situation. It validates every person's perspective and involves each person in reaching a resolution. It transforms conflict into cooperation, thereby changing an adversarial culture into a cooperative one. Although some versions can be time-consuming and involve heavy manpower, it can be extremely successful. The secret is in using a properly trained convener to run it fairly.[13]

Mediation

> We do not treat a physical injury as a matter to be mediated. We ask for the causes to be fixed. Mediation as a proposed resolution runs the risk of putting the onus on the victim, while allowing the organisation to be seen to be doing something about an incident without accepting much responsibility.

Some companies instigate a mediation or dispute resolution process first, others do it following their investigation. Both targets and bullies are entitled to have their union representative, lawyer or other support person to assist them. Mediation is an informal structure to resolve the conflict. It is designed as a nonadversarial process, based on openness, voluntary participation and confidentiality. It should use trained staff or professional mediators; however, the outcome is decided by the parties, not the facilitator.

Beware that mediation processes can be a disaster waiting to happen in the case of workplace bullying.[14] Unfortunately, standard conflict resolution methods exacerbate a target's powerlessness and increase the likelihood of a bully retaliating. This process reflects the organisation's intention to end the dispute, rather than their desire for justice or improving productivity. It also focuses on the current conflict rather than on past bullying behaviours, the work climate, culture, any mobbing, the bully's other behaviours, and neglects the systemic picture. Thus it is less appropriate where there are power imbalances — supervisor to employee, or a serial bully and a traumatised target — or when the target lacks the assertive skills to confront the bully within the mediation.

Investigation

The traditional approach following a formal complaint is to conduct an investigation. An employer should use trained, experienced investigators, whose final decision is based upon the balance of probabilities. External investigators are more suitable for small companies, sensitive areas, strong personalities, when the bully is the target's manager, or when someone with special expertise is required during and after the investigation. Unfortunately, some investigators have a poor understanding of what workplace bullying actually involves, the damage it causes everywhere at work and the difficulty of obtaining all the evidence when some is camouflaged. They conduct unjust, unfair, inadequate, biased appraisals, thereby making investigations even more stressful.[15]

Conciliation

Conciliation generally follows an investigation and constitutes a formal structure where each person needs to be advised of their options and rights. The conciliator's decision is also based on the balance of probabilities, that is, whether the bullying behaviours would affect a reasonable person. They use a civil, not criminal, standard of proof. They need expert knowledge of dispute resolution processes, careful preparation and detailed documentation. They should understand the causes and damage created by workplace bullying and identify overt or covert manipulative behaviours adopted by targets, bullies, bystanders and managers. The conciliator evaluates, guides, and makes a confidential, legally binding decision.

Courts and tribunals

Most employers are relieved when a victim leaves, but the matter may not end there. In some cases targets take legal action, immediately or later on. Although employers may fantasise that if they proceed with legal action they can leave everything to their lawyers, numerous staff have to find the information (such as employment records and performance reviews), obtain statutory declarations from witnesses and attend court. Although employers may afford top barristers to ruin a victim's testimony, they can lose too. Apart from the obvious legal costs, time in court and administration costs for one target or a class action, employers can be damaged by poor publicity, threatened by unions, sued by a government department or pursued by the police.

Some organisations learn from their blind spots and take action to reduce bullying and prevent further injuries. Unfortunately, the main cause of bullying, a dysfunctional management system, remains unchanged if employers maintain a blind spot to the connection between their legal, administration and other financial costs and bullying, thereby further sabotaging employees and productivity.

Step 11: Implement consequences

> *John confronted Malcolm, his manager, 'I find your behaviour offensive, please don't do it again'. Malcolm continued but his own manager wasn't impressed. Despite being very senior, Malcolm lost a promotion and had to attend an anger management training program.*

Organisations need to apply appropriate consequences for bullying behaviours in line with their legal and ethical obligations. Just like school students, employees need to know the behaviour boundaries and the consequences of not respecting them. When a bully escapes disciplinary action, receives a promotion or an excellent reference to move on, the organisation is seen as rewarding bullying, which institutionalises bullying behaviours.

In addition, targets, bullies and witnesses need protection for filing a complaint or assisting an investigation; thus sanctions are required for any type of retaliation. Even sociopaths understand that unacceptable behaviours have serious consequences. These sanctions should be advertised widely, so that bullies receive clear warnings about penalties, otherwise an employer can sack a bully, lose in court because s/he was not warned, and be forced to return the bully to the same department!

Possible consequences for bullying include:

- a fine for negative comment — a dollar for charity
- an apology in writing (public or private)
- a written or verbal warning
- discussion regarding performance management
- training, coaching, mentoring, counselling or therapy

- restorative practices, mediation or conciliation
- a temporary stand-down or suspension
- withdrawal of privileges
- transfer to another department
- demotion to a lower status position
- loss of pay or promotion
- termination of employment.

Step 12: Rehabilitate and restore

> *'Since attending the return-to-work group, my interview skills have improved. When I saw myself on the video recorder, I knew that I need to appear more positive and get rid of the nasty bully's voice which puts me down and takes away my confidence.'*

> *Fred worked in an engineering team. He felt very hurt and powerless when they bullied him. When the HR department organised a meeting, Fred said the bullies 'dished out crap'. He called them 'slime balls and sleazebuckets'. Although the bullying stopped, Fred had lost respect for the bullies and couldn't work with them. He moved to another team.*

When employees are injured physically they receive flowers or balloons and caring phone calls from their employer or his representative. Similarly, any employee who requires time off work following bullying needs regular, supportive contact from their workplace. They may require rehabilitation, a graduated return to work and training to update their job skills, counselling to recover from the bullying and rebuild their shattered self-confidence, and skills to block future bullies.

Whether or not some employees move away or leave, the work climate will not automatically return to its prebullying state when the bullying conflict ends. Many employees will feel distressed or threatened before, during or after the dispute intervention processes; thus some form of psychological debriefing or other reconstructive strategies are advisable. Everyone can be affected by the toxic experience, especially if the target and bully have to continue working together. Staff need assistance to welcome, support and include anyone who has been away from work due to bullying. Rebuilding the team could involve a training day (preferably away from the office) to reintegrate everyone, help them move on from the toxic relationships and resume teamwork. A session could include acknowledgment, shared feelings, feedback, team skills to begin again, and perhaps a closure ritual. The goal is help every employee return to work and rebuild effective working relationships. Retraining and counselling referrals can be far more economical than distressed or disenfranchised employees who take extended sick leave or quit, high staff turnover, and organisational mistakes.

Step 13: Review and monitor regularly

> Scott said that a 360-degree feedback program was instituted to prevent further bullying at his company. However, everyone is too scared to say how they feel about anyone else. Scott can't tell his boss that he's weak and allows the bully to walk over everyone. He needs his boss to protect him. No-one rocks the boat and dobbing isn't allowed. He said that values are zilch in his company, even though signs are plastered everywhere!

Reducing and eliminating workplace bullying is a huge challenge. Organisations that are committed to reducing bullying need to regularly review and monitor their policies, procedures and programs at all levels to ensure their commitment is not watered down over time. This process can include feedback to a taskforce to review and take further action.

Methods of review include: casual chats (e.g., *How's the work culture now?*), monitoring sick leave, absenteeism and staff turnover rates, exit interviews, staff attitude or climate surveys, performance appraisals, employee satisfaction (using suggestion boxes, telephones), anonymous feedback, focus groups, grievance procedures, emails, complaints and resolutions.

Conclusion:
Respect and resilience

Thirty years ago no-one worried about working in a cigarette smoke-filled workplace, and the concept of metal detectors in schools and airports was inconceivable. Today in some countries, domestic violence and school bullying attract criminal, legal and welfare interventions.

Things do change. If you are working in an organisation where bullying is denied or minimised, where workers are regularly subjected to public abuse and humiliation by aggressive managers who shout obscenities or passive managers turn a blind eye, there is light at the end of the tunnel. Although workplace bullying is treated differently in different countries, the overall picture has been improving in the past decade.

The media, quick to reflect new trends, is using the word *bullying* more and more often in relation to adults. People are becoming aware that workplace bullying is destructive and unproductive. The internet and social networking sites are also publicising what is fair, possible and appropriate.

Public awareness leads to legislative change and although it is very difficult for most targets to achieve justice, eventually there will be an increase in legislation to reduce and regulate this toxic phenomenon. Organisations will be encouraged to respect their employees, improve leadership and their cultures, as well as manage workplace bullying with respect and collaboration. Hopefully, the legal, welfare, medical and mental health professions will discover more appropriate ways to help every employee develop their social and emotional resilience to survive at work and improve their working relationships.

Now I invite you to join me in educating, mentoring and managing others so that workplaces can become safer, more productive and enjoyable. Thank you for reading this book and sharing with me some of the issues that can make this world a better place.

Evelyn M. Field, FAPS

Endnotes

Chapter 2

1   Workplace violence: 'Incidents where staff are abused, threatened or assaulted in circumstances related to their work, including commuting to and from work, involving an explicit or implicit challenge to their safety, well being or health.' Richards, J. (2003). *International Labour Office (ILO), Joint Programme on Workplace Violence in the Health Sector*, Geneva.

2   The description of workplace bullying is based upon the research by Stale Einarson and a subsequent discussion with Paul McCarthy, to which I have added my own ideas.

3   Mobbing — There is debate whether mobbing solely represents a translation of the word *bullying* or describes bullying by a group. I am using it to describe the latter. Research into mobbing was pioneered in the 1980s by German-born Swedish scientist Heinz Leymann. See Herriot, P., Zapf, D., & Leymann, H. (1996). Mobbing and victimization at work. *European Journal of Work and Organizational Psychology, 5*(2) 161–164. Refer to the website www.leymann.se

4   'Hazing refers to any activity expected of someone joining a group (or maintain full group status) that humiliates, degrades or risks emotional and/or physical harm, regardless of the person's willingness to participate.' Refer to www.stophazing.org

5   Lennane, J. (1995, November). *The canary down the mine: what whistleblowers' health tells us about their environment.* Paper presented at Whistleblowers: Protecting the Nation's Conscience? Conference, Department of Criminology, Melbourne University, Australia.

6   According to the experts Stale Einarson and Dieter Zapf there are five main areas where bullying occurs. See Einarsen, S., Hoel, H.Z.D., Zapf, D., & Cooper, G.L. (2003). *Bullying and emotional abuse in the workplace.* London and New York: Taylor & Francis.

7   Prevalence of bullying — one in six children in Australia bullied weekly. Rigby, K. (2002). *A meta-evaluation of methods and approaches to reducing bullying in pre-schools and in early primary school in Australia.* Canberra, Australia: Commonwealth Attorney-General's Department.

8   See Hoel, H., Cooper, C., & Faragher, B. (2001). The experience of bullying in Great Britain: The impact of organisational status. *European of Work and Organizational Psychology, 10*(4) 443–465); See also Rayner C. (1997). *Bullying at work, bullying survey report.* London: UNISON.

9   Branch, S., Sheehan, M.J., Ramsay, S.G., & Barker, M.C. (2004). *Upwards bullying: Implications for how managers and organisations approach workplace bullying in the future.* Paper presented at British Academy of Management, St Andrews.

10 Bullying Behaviours Checklist — refer Cartwright, S., & Cooper, C.L. (2007). Hazards to health: The problem of workplace bullying, *The Psychologist, 20*(5), 284–286.

Chapter 3

1   See Burger, M. (2009). Replicating Milgram: Would people still obey today? *American Psychologist, 64,* 1–11.

2   Although 'prisoners' showed severe emotional distress and powerlessness, they obeyed the rules. Other wardens did nothing. This experiment was planned for 2 weeks but terminated after 6 days because of the dramatic changes in personality and behaviours shown by the students, which were first identified when Christina, Phillip's girlfriend visited him and became horrified. They later married!

3   Zimbardo, P.G. (2004). A situationist perspective on the psychology of evil: Understanding how good people are transformed into perpetrators. In A.G. Miller (Ed.), *The social psychology of good and evil* (pp. 21–50). New York: Guilford Press.

4   'Psychopaths are social predators who charm, manipulate, and ruthlessly plow their way through life, leaving a broad trail of broken hearts, shattered expectations, and empty wallets. Completely lacking in conscience and feelings for others, they selfishly take what they want and do as they please, violating social norms and expectations without the slightest sense of guilt or regret'. Hare, R. (1993). *Without conscience: The disturbing world of psychopaths among us.* New York: Guildford Press.

5   See www.hare.org/. Professor Robert D. Hare, University of Columbia, has spent over 35 years researching psychopathy and developed the Hare Psychopathy Checklist-Revised (PCL-R). He is a co-author of the Guidelines for a Psychopathy Treatment Program.

6   Tim Field was a victim of workplace bullying and edited *Bully in sight: How to predict, resist, challenge and combat workplace bullying* (1996, published by Success Unlimited), the first book to identify the serial bully at work. The term for this type of bully includes employees who are psychopaths, sociopaths or have antisocial personality disorders, and those who systematically abuse power.

7   See Crawshaw, L. (2007). *Taming the abrasive manager: How to end unnecessary roughness in the workplace* (Jossey-Bass Management Series). San Francisco: Jossey-Bass.

8   See Field, E.M. (1999). *Bully busting.* Sydney, Australia: Finch Publishing; and Field, E.M. (2007). *Bully blocking.* Sydney, Australia: Finch Publishing.

9   See Oakley, C.A. (1945). *Men at work: Industrial psychology in the factory.* London: University of London Press.

10 See Brodsky, C. (1976). *The harassed worker.* Lexington, MA: Lexington Books.

11 There are many others around the world who are contributing to research and practice, including Mona O'Moore, Jean Lynch (Ireland), Judith Marais-Steinman (South Africa), Pat Ferris (Canada) Angelo Soars, Marie-France Hirigoyen (France), Renato Gilioli (Italy), Eva Gemzoe Mikkelsen (Denmark), Maarit Vartia (Finland), Shayne Mathieson and Hayden Olsen (New Zealand).

12 See Cotton, P., & Hart, P. (2003). Occupational wellbeing and performance: A review of organisational research. *Australian Psychologist, 38*(2), 118–128.

Chapter 4

1   Organisational causes — according to Einarson (in an email to the author) the original reference was Leymann, H., (1993), *Mobbing: Psychoterror am Arbeitsplatz und wie man sich dagegen wehren kann.* Hamberg: Verlag. Einarson has written further about it in numerous places, such as his 1999 article in *Journal of Manpower,* in the book *Bullying and emotional abuse in the workplace* (2003) and in Bowie, V., Fisher, B.S., & Cooper, C.L. (2005). *Workplace violence: Issues, trends, strategies.* Portland, OR: Willan Publishing.

2   Gare, S. (2009, January 30). Bullying: Secret women's business. *The Weekend Australian Magazine.*

3   McCarthy, P., Sheehan, M., & Kearns, D. (1995). *Managerial styles and their effect on employees' health and well-being in organisations undergoing restructuring.* Brisbane, Australia: Griffith University, School of Organisational Behaviour and Human Resource Management.

4   Ferris, P. (2004). A preliminary typology of organisational response to allegations of workplace bullying: See no evil, hear no evil, speak no evil. *British Journal of Guidance & Counselling, 32*(3), 389–395.

5   Jones, E.E., & Davis, K.E. (1965). From acts to dispositions: The attribution process in social psychology. In L. Berkowitz (Ed.), *Advances in experimental social psychology* (Vol. 2, pp. 219–266), New York: Academic Press.

6   Lynch, J., & Kilmartin, C. (1999). *The pain behind the mask: Overcoming masculine depression.* London: Haworth Press.

7   Steinman, S.M. (2002, February). *Workplace violence in the health sector: A country case study of South Africa.* Paper presented at the Adelaide International Workplace Bullying Conference, Australia.

8   According to information provided at www.workplacebullying.org, Drs Ruth and Gary Namie believe that legislation in the United States deals with the 1 in 130,000 people who are at risk of work homicide, the 1 in 25 at risk of physical violence, and the 1 in 9 people at risk of illegal harassment and discrimination, but there is far less legislation for the 1 in 6 who risk psychological and verbal violence.

9   Rayner, C. (1997). *Bullying at work, bullying survey report.* London: UNISON.

10 Gettler, L. (2005). *Organisations behaving badly: A Greek tragedy of corporate pathology.* Brisbane, Australia: John Wiley & Sons.

11 Lennane, J. (1995). *The canary down the mine: What whistleblowers' health tells us about their environment.* Paper presented at Whistleblowers: Protecting the nation's conscience? Conference, Department of Criminology, Melbourne University, Australia.

12 Cortina, L.M., & Magley, V.J. (2003). Raising voice, risking retaliation: Events following interpersonal mistreatment in the workplace. *Journal of Occupational Health Psychology, 8,* 247–265.

Chapter 5

1 Eisenberger, N.I., Lieberman, M.D, & Williams, K.D. (2003). Does rejection hurt? An MRI Study of Social Exclusion, *Science, 302,* 290–292.

> Social connection is so essential to survival that being left out or disconnected from the social group is processed by the brain in a manner similar to physical pain. Just as physical pain has evolved to alert us that 'something has gone wrong' with our bodies, social pain is a similarly potent signal that alerts us when 'something has gone wrong with our social connections to others, an equally important threat to the survival of our species'. ... The anterior cingulate cortex (ACC), a large structure on the medial wall of the frontal lobe, is one of the key neural structures involved in the affective distress associated with the physical–social pain overlap. The ACC seems to be involved in registering the distress as opposed to the intensity of physical pain. ACC is involved in physical pain but also in social pain, resulting from social distance or separation.

2 See Ebert, A., & M. J. Dyck (2004). The experience of mental death: The core feature of complex posttraumatic stress disorder. *Clinical Psychology Review, 24,* 617–635.

3 Janoff-Bulman, R. (1992). *Shattered assumptions: Towards a new psychology of trauma.* New York: Free Press. Refer chapter 8.

4 Namie, G., & Namie, R. (2000). *The bully at work.* Naperville, IL: Source Books.

5 See Einarsen, S., Hoel, H.Z.D., Zapf, D., & Cooper, G.L. (2003) *Bullying and emotional abuse in the workplace.* London and New York: Taylor & Francis.

6 See Einarsen, S., Hoel, H.Z.D., Zapf, D., & Cooper, G.L. (2003) *Bullying and emotional abuse in the workplace.* London and New York: Taylor & Francis.

7 See Einarsen, S., Hoel, H.Z.D., Zapf, D., & Cooper, G.L. (2003) *Bullying and emotional abuse in the workplace.* London and New York: Taylor & Francis.

8 See Hjortskov, N., Garde, A.H., Ørbæk, P., & Hansen, Å.M. (2004). Evaluation of salivary cortisol as a biomarker of self-reported mental stress in field studies. *Stress and Health, 20,* 91–98.

9 Soares, A. (2004). *Bullying, PTSD and social support.* Paper presented at the Fourth International Conference on Bullying and Harassment, Norway.

10 Yehuda, R., Teicher, M.H., Trestman, R.L., Levengood, R.A., & Siever, LJ. (1996). Cortisol regulation in posttraumatic stress disorder and major depression: A chronobiological analysis. *Biology Psychiatry, 40,* 79–88.

11 Barling, J. (1998). Bullying in the workplace is a violence warning sign. *APA Monitor, 29*(7). Available at http://www.apa.org/monitor/Jul98/bully.html

12 Goleman, D. (2006, September 3). Can you raise your social IQ? *Parade Magazine.* Available at http://www.parade.com/articles/editions/2006/edition_09-03-2006/Social_Intelligence. Based upon this article: Empathy and social skills are the two main ingredients of social intelligence. This includes being able to read a situation to know how to make a good impression and being able to sense another's feelings and intentions as rejection causes pain. Social IQ has a real impact in the workplace. Australian researchers found that workers recall a boss's downbeat comments far more often, in greater detail and with more intensity than they do his encouraging words. When negative remarks become a preoccupation, that worker's brain loses mental efficiency.

13 Maslow, A. (1962). *Toward a psychology of being.* Princeton, NJ: D. Van Nostrand Co.

14 Collis, G. (2002, March). Introduction to the Adelaide International Workplace Bullying Conference, Adelaide, Australia.

15 Raynor, C. (2000, September). *Building a business case for tacking bullying in the workplace: Beyond a basic cost–benefit approach.* Paper presented to the 'Transcending Boundaries' conference, Brisbane, Australia.

16 Rayner, C., Hoel, H., & Cooper, G. (2002). *Workplace bullying: What we know, who is to blame and what can we do?* London: Taylor Francis.

17 Canada Safety Council. (2000.) Report on bullying in the workplace. *Safety Canada, 4*, 7–8.

18 Watson, C., & Hoffman, L.R. (1996). Managers as negotiators: A test of power versus gender as predictors of success. *Leadership Quarterly, 7*(1), 63–85.

19 Ilies, R., Hauserman, N., Schowochau, S., & Stibal, J. (2003). Reported incidence rates of work-related sexual harassment in the United States: Using meta-analysis to explain reported rate disparities. *Personnel Psychology, 56*, 607–631.

20 Johnson, P., & Indvik, J. (1996). Stress and violence in the workplace. *Journal of Workplace Learning, 8*(1), 19–24.

21 Browne, R. (2008, August 17). Y this generation jumps jobs. *The Age.*

22 Caminiti, S. (2005). Fortune, a new health care prescription. *APA Monitor on Psychology, 36*(4).

23 Australian Government Productivity Commission. (200). *Performance benchmarking of Australian business regulation: Occupational health and safe*ty (Draft research report). Available at http://www.pc.gov.au/__data/assets/pdf_file/ 0003/94350/13chapter11.pdf

24 Munsey, C. (2006). Health workplaces lauded. *APA Monitor on Psychology, 37*(5). Available at www.apa.org/monitor/may06/workplaces.html

25 Hoel, H., Sparks, K., & Cooper, C.L. (2001). The cost of violence stress at work and the benefits of a violence/stress-free working environment (Report commissioned by the International Labour Organization (ILO). Geneva: ILO.

26 Namie, G., & Namie, R. (2009). *The bully at work.* Naperville, IL: Source Books.

27 Olsen, H. (2005). *Workplace bullying and harassment.* New Zealand: CCH New Zealand Ltd.

28 Chappel, D., & Di Martino, V. (2006). *Violence at work.* Geneva: International Labour Organization.

29 Sheehan, M., McCarthy, P., Barker, M., & Henderson, M. (Workplace Bullying Project Team, Griffith University, Queensland). (2001, June–July). *A model for assessing the impacts and costs of workplace bullying, Griffith University.* Paper presented at The Standing Conference on Organizational Symbolism, SCOS XIX Conference, Trinity College, Dublin.
The estimated prevalence rates of workplace bullying in Scandinavia (3.5%) appear lower than the estimated prevalence rates (15%) in the United Kinggdom, the United States and Australia. This could be due to more subtle, less obvious bullying which is harder to quantify, cultural differences or different research tools.

Chapter 7

1   Frankl, V. (1959). *Man's search for meaning*. New York: Simon and Schuster.

2   Namie, R. Personal communication.

3   Campbell, J. (1968). *The hero with a thousand faces*. Princeton University Press.

4   Field, E.M. (1999). *Bully busting*. Sydney, Australia: Finch Publishing.

Chapter 8

1   Adams, A., & Crawford, N. (1992). *Bullying at work: How to confront and overcome it*. London: Virago.

2   Hunter, M. (Speaker). (April 19, 2007). *PTSD: Treatment and the brain*. Toronto, ON.

3   Fournier, J.C., DeRubeis, R.J., Hollon, S.D., Dimidjian, S., Amsterdam, J.D., Shelton, R.C. et al. (2010). Antidepressant drug effects and depression severity: A patient-level meta-analysis. *Journal of the American Medical Association, 303*(1).

4   Silberman, S. (2009). *Placebos are getting more effective. Drugmakers are desperate to know why*. Available at www.wired.com

5   Janoff-Bulman, R. (1985). The aftermath of victimization: Rebuilding shattered assumptions. In C.R. Figley (Ed.), *Trauma and its wake: The study and treatment of posttraumatic stress disorder* (pp. 15–35). New York: Brunner/Mazel Inc.

Janoff-Bulman explains the processes involved in recovering from trauma:

> Whenever someone becomes victimized by a disaster, whatever its nature, their most basic assumptions about themselves and the world are undermined. The key assumption that crumbles in a disaster is that of invulnerability, the sense that the world is benevolent, controllable and fair, and that so long as one acts as one should, nothing untoward will happen. These beliefs are at the core of a person's most basic sense of himself and the world … A catastrophe attacks those deeply held beliefs, suddenly all the world seems malevolent. And because the two beliefs are so intimately linked, you lose not only your sense that the world is safe for you, but that you are worthy of that safety … When you've been victimized, it leads you to ask, 'Why me?' That leads you to highlight the negative aspects of yourself, which lowers your self-esteem. Psychological recovery, to a large extent, requires rebuilding those assumptions.

Chapter 9

1   Tracy, S.J., Alberts, J.K., & Rivera, K.D. (2009). How to bust the office bully: Eight tactics for explaining workplace abuse to decision-makers. In A. Varma (Ed.), *Understanding and addressing workplace bullying*. Andhra Pradesh, India: ICFAI University Press.

2   Patricia, F. (2004). A preliminary typology of organisational response to allegations of workplace bullying: See no evil, hear no evil, speak no evil. *British Journal of Guidance & Counselling, 32*(3).

3   Author's communication with David Moore of Conflict Management Constructive Communication.

Refer Moore, D.B., (2004). Managing social conflict — the evolution of a practical theory. *Journal of Sociology and Social Work, 31*(1), 71–91.

4   In what is understood to be an Australian first, a company has been convicted in relation to verbal harassment of staff by a colleague. At the Victorian government web site www.worksafe.vic.gov.au it was reported that:

> Ballarat Radio Pty Ltd pleaded guilty to a series of incidents between February 2000 and October last year. The company was convicted and fined $25,000 for failing to provide a safe workplace, and $25,000 for failing to provide instruction, training and supervision in relation to bullying. It was also ordered to pay costs of $5,000. Mr Mowat appeared in the Ballarat Magistrates Court on July 22 in relation to occupational health and safety charges laid as a result of his bullying behaviour. He was convicted, fined $10,000 and ordered to pay costs of $1700.

Chapter 10

1   Gorman, P. (1998). Bullying, a legal response. In McCarthy, P., Sheehan, M., Wilkie, S., & Wilkie, W. (Eds.) *Bullying, causes, costs and cures.* Brisbane, Australia: Beyond Bullying Association.

2   See Coid, J., Yang, M., Tyrer, P., Roberts, A., & Ullrich, S. (2006). Prevalence and correlates of personality disorder in Great Britain. *The British Journal of Psychiatry, 188,* 423–431.

3   Cooper, J. (Ed.). (1992). *ICD 10 Classification of Mental and Behavioural Disorders.* Geneva: World Health Organization.

4   Leymann, H., & Gustafsson, A. (1996). Mobbing at work and the development of post-traumatic stress disorders. *European Journal of Work and Organizational Psychology, 5,* 251–276.

5   Kupfer, D.J., First, M.B., & Regier, D.A. (2002). *A research agenda for DSM–V.* Washington, DC: American Psychiatric Association:

> [Relational disorder] is the juncture or bond between or among the members of a relationship that is disordered. The disorder cannot be reduced to an individual diagnosis of any member and its consequent impact on others … Relational disorders are persistent and painful patterns of feelings, behavior, and perceptions involving two or more partners in an important long-standing, corrosive relationship with clear evidence of a major impact of these patterns on psychological functioning, physical health, social adaptation, and/or occupational effectiveness in one or both partners.

6   American Psychiatric Association. (2000). *Diagnostic and Statistical Manual of Mental Disorders (DSM-IV-TR)* states:

> The person has been exposed to a traumatic event in which both of the following were present: Criterion 1. The person experienced, witnessed, or was confronted with an event or events that involved actual or threatened death or serious injury, or a threat to the physical integrity of self or others. Criterion 2. The person's response involved intense fear, helplessness, or horror.

7   De Maria, W. (1996). *Bullying from backyard to boardroom.* Brisbane, Australia: Workplace Bullying Project Team, Griffith University.

8   Linnane, Jean. (1996). Bullying in medico–legal examinations. In McCarthy, P. (Ed.), *Bullying: From backyard to boardroom.* Sydney, Australia: Millenium Books.

9 Harper, A. (1999). *The tomb of the unknown worker, when psychiatric fiction becomes litigants' lives. Responding to professional abuse.* Paper presented at the Third International Conference, Brisbane.

10 Australian Centre for Posttraumatic Mental Health. (2007). *Guidelines for the treatment of adults with acute stress disorder and posttraumatic stress disorder: Practitioner guide.* Melbourne, Australia: Author.

11 Cortisol testing — research stage. See Yehuda, R., Yehuda, R., Kahana, B., Binder-Brynes, K., Southwick, S.M., Mason, J.W., & Giller, E.L. (1995). Low urinary cortisol excretion in Holocaust survivors with posttraummatic stress disorder. *American Journal of Psychiatry, 152*(7), 982–986. See also Yehuda, R., Teicher, M.H., Trestman, R.L., Levengood, R.A., & Siever, L.J. (1996). Cortisol regulation in posttraumatic stress disorder and major depression: A chronobiological analysis. *Biology Psychiatry, 40,* 79–88.

12 World Health Organization, (1992). *The ICD-10 Classification of Mental and Behavioural Disorders.* Geneva: Author.

13 PDM Task Force. (2006). *Psychodynamic diagnostic manual.* Silver Spring, MD: Alliance of Psychoanalytic Organizations.

14 Romano, C.J. (2004). *Posttraumatic stress disorder: A continuing controversy in neuropsychiatry.* Available at www.neuropsychiatryreviews.com. According to Rachel Yehuda:

> Factors such as the degree of perceived controllability and predictability, plus feelings of shame, humiliation, guilt, and the sense that one could have prevented what happened and minimized damage and injury to others, could be important determinants…. The problem in posttraumatic stress disorder is understanding why the person still has biologic reactions to an event that has long since stopped occurring. The reaction to stress is biological, but it is fundamentally influenced by what you think at the time of the trauma, which is influenced by pre-trauma factors, which is influenced by cultural factors.'

15 Herman, J.L. (1992). Complex PTSD: A syndrome in survivors of prolonged and repeated trauma. *Journal of Traumatic Stress, 5*(3), 377–391.
   According to the National Center for Posttraumatic Stress Disorder (www.ptsd. va.gov) the current PTSD diagnosis does not always capture the severe psychological harm that occurs with prolonged, repeated trauma. Research is currently underway to determine if the complex PTSD diagnosis is the best way to categorise the symptoms of patients who have suffered prolonged trauma.

16 Since the next major revision of the *Diagnostic and Statistical Manual of Mental Disorders (DSM-V)* will not appear until 2013 (i.e., at least 19 years after DSM-IV was published in 1994), a text revision of DSM-IV, called DSM-IV-TR, was published by the American Psychiatric Association in July 2000.

17 Yehuda, R., Teicher, M.H., Trestman, R.L., Levengood, R.A., & Siever, L.J. (1996). Cortisol regulation in posttraumatic stress disorder and major depression: A chronobiological analysis. *Biology Psychiatry, 40,* 79–88.

18 Hansen, A.M., Hogh, A., Persson, R., Karlson, B., Garde, A.H., Ørbaek, P. et al. (2006). Bullying at work, health outcomes, and physiological stress response. *Journal of Psychosomatic Research, 60,* 63–72.

19 Eisenberger, N.I., Lieberman, M.D, & Williams, K.D. (2003). Does rejection hurt? An MRI Study of Social Exclusion, *Science, 302,* 290–292.

20 Ozer, E.J., Best, S.R., Lipsey, T.L., & Weiss, D.S. (2003). Predictors of posttraumatic stress disorder and symptoms in adults; A meta analysis. *Psychological Bulletin, 129*(1), 52–73.

21 Van Hooff, M., McFarlane, A.C., Baur, J., Abraham, M., & Barne, D.J. (2009). The stressor Criterion-A1 and PTSD: A matter of opinion? *Journal of Anxiety Disorders, 23*(1), 77–86:

> Considerable controversy exists with regard to the interpretation and definition of the stressor 'A1' criterion for Post Traumatic Stress Disorder (PTSD). At present, classifying an event as either traumatic (satisfying DSM-IV Criterion-A1 for PTSD), or non-traumatic (life event) is determined by the rater's subjective interpretation of the diagnostic criteria. This has implications in research and clinical practice. Utilizing a sample of 860 Australian adults, this study is the first to provide a detailed examination of the impact of event categorization on the prevalence of trauma and PTSD. Overall, events classified as non-traumatic were associated with higher rates of PTSD. Unanimous agreement between raters occurred for 683 (79.4%) events. As predicted, the categorization method employed (single rater, multiple rater-majority, multiple rater-unanimous) substantially altered the prevalence of Criterion-A1 events and PTSD, raising doubts about the functionality of PTSD diagnostic criteria.

22 Ebert, A., & Dyck, M.J. (2004). The experience of mental death: The core feature of complex posttraumatic stress disorder. *Clinical Psychology Review, 24,* 617–635.

23 Letter to author from Dr George Halascz, psychiatrist and Holocaust expert.

24 Posttraumatic embitterment disorder (PTED), developed by Prof Michael Linden (2003) Germany and researched by Dr Harold Ege (Italy) with victims of workplace bullying. Embitterment can occur if basic beliefs (in respect to justice) are violated, triggered by a single event. It is associated with emotional arousal, intrusive memories, sleep disorders, depression, social and affective impairment, loss of self-esteem, psychosomatic symptoms, and it affects daily living.

25 Australian Centre for Posttraumatic Mental Health. (2007). *Australian Guidelines for the Treatment of Adults with Acute Stress Disorder and Posttraumatic Stress Disorder.* Melbourne, Australia: Author.

Questionnaire based upon scale developed by Breslau, N., Peterson, E., Kessler, R., & Schultz, L. (1999). Short Screening Scale for DSM-IV posttraumatic stress disorder. *American Journal of Psychiatry, 156,* 908–911. This screening measure has been empirically validated:

1. Do you avoid being reminded of the experience by staying away from certain places, people or activities?
2. Have you lost interest in activities that were once important or enjoyable?
3. Have you begun to feel more distant or isolated from other people?
4. Do you find it hard to feel love or affection for other people?
5. Have you begun to feel that there is no point in planning for the future?
6. Have you had more trouble than usual falling or staying asleep?
7. Do you become jumpy or easily startled by ordinary noise or movements?

If a person answers *Yes* to four or more of these questions, a PTSD diagnosis is likely.

26 In 2009, I shared correspondence and examples of evidence with Dr Mathew Friedman, the DSM-V Trauma Committee chairperson, about the inclusion of workplace bullying as a possible cause of trauma.

27 Tehrani, N. (2004). Bullying: A source of chronic post-traumatic stress? *British Journal of Guidance & Counselling, 32*(3), 357–366.

28 Meewisse, M-L., Reitsma, J.B., De Vries, G-J., Gersons, B.P.R., & Olff, M. (2007). Cortisol and post-traumatic stress disorder in adults, systematic review and meta-analysis. *British Journal of Psychiatry, 191,* 387–392.

29 See Leyman & Gustaffsson (1996), Mobbing at work and the development of post-traumatic stress disorders. *European Journal of Work and Organizational Psychology, 5,* 119–126.

30 Yamada, D. (2003). Workplace bullying and the law. Einarsen, S., Hoel, H.Z.D., Zapf, D., & Cooper, G.L. (2003) *Bullying and emotional abuse in the workplace* (p. 405). London and New York: Taylor and Francis.

Chapter 11

1 Safety Canada. (2000). *There is no place for bullies in a well-run organization,* Available at http://archive.safety-council.org/info/OSH/bullies.html

2 Sapolsky, R. (2004). Emergence of a peaceful culture in wild baboons. *PLoS Biol* 2: e106. Available at www.plosbiology.org

3 Anna Miller-Tiedeman, A. (1999). *Learning, practicing, and living the new careering.* Philadelphia: Taylor Francis Group.

4 Testimony from Smith, M. (2003). In *Report of the Columbia Accident Investigation Board, Vol. I.* Available at www.gpo.gov. www.nasa.gov/columbia.

5 Pederson, H. (2004). *The need for a legal perspective in cases that involve escalated conflicts and/or bullying.* Paper presented at the Fourth International Conference on Bullying and Harassment in the Workplace, Norway.

6 Cross, D. (2006, May). *Helping to make schools safer, where policy meets playground.* Paper presented at the National Coalition Against Bullying, Melbourne, Australia. Cross quoted Signe Maria Natvig Andreassen, a principal from Gran School, Norway.

7 Richards, J., & Daley, H. (2003). Bullying policy: Development, implementation, and monitoring. Einarsen, S., Hoel, H.Z.D., Zapf, D., & Cooper, G.L. (2003) *Bullying and emotional abuse in the workplace* (pp. 247–258). London: Taylor & Francis.

8 Mathieson, S, Burns, J., & Hansen, M. (2006). *Reducing the risk of harassment in your organization.* Wellington, New Zealand: Top Drawer Consultants.

9 Training questionnaire based on conference presentation by Einarson, S. (2000, September). *Bullying and harassment at work, unveiling an organizational taboo.* Paper presented at the 'Transcending Boundaries,' conference, Brisbane, Australia

10 Mathieson, S., Burns, J., & Hansen, M. (2006). *Reducing the risk of harassment in your organization.* Wellington, New Zealand: Top Drawer Consultants.

11 Woods, M. (2003). *Inquiry into National Worker's Compensation and Occupational Health and Safety Frameworks,* Productivity Commission, Melbourne, Australia.

12 Tehrani, N. Shaw, R., & Peyron, D. (2008, June). *Dignity at work advisors.* Paper presented at Creating Dignity in the Workplace, 6th International Conference on Workplace Bullying, Sharing our Knowledge, Montreal.

13 Personal communication with David Moore, consultant in communication and organisational change.

14 Merchant, V., & Hoel, H. (2003). Investigating complaints of bullying. In Einarsen, S., Hoel, H.Z.D., Zapf, D., & Cooper, G.L. (2003) *Bullying and emotional abuse in the workplace* (pp. 259–269). London and New York: Taylor and Francis.

15 Ferris, P. (2004). A preliminary typology of organisational response to allegations of workplace bullying: See no evil, hear no evil, speak no evil. *British Journal of Guidance & Counselling, 32*(3), 389–395.

About the Author

Evelyn M. Field is a Fellow of the Australian Psychological Society, a practising psychologist, professional speaker, author, and well-known Australian media psychologist.

She is on the Board of the National Centre Against Bullying and spent 5 years on the Board of VOCAL (Victims of Crime Assistance League, Victoria), 20 years as a Board Member of the Mental Health Foundation of Victoria, and 11 years as Honorary Secretary of the Australian Association for Mental Health. She was an Accredited Speaking Member of National Speakers Association and has spoken in New Zealand, Belgium, Spain, USA, Vietnam and Israel.

Evelyn's unique presentations are entertaining, ethical and educational, and have been given to adolescents, parents, teachers, health professionals and organisations. She uses a variety of techniques, including case studies, stories, cartoons, magic, and role-playing, to engage participants and help them learn and develop new skills. The core of her training is based upon a social survival skills model derived from her personal and professional experience.

Bully Busting, Evelyn's first self-help book for parents, children and educators sold over 23,000 copies and has been translated into Italian, Croatian and Arabic. Her follow-up, *Bully Blocking* — also a bestseller — has been translated into Czechoslovakian and Korean. She also wrote a chapter entitled 'Parenting for Bullying Solutions' for the National Coalition Against Bullying.

Evelyn provides keynotes and workshops across Australia and overseas on:

- 'Understanding and Managing Workplace Bullying, or Developing Respect and Resilience at Work' — for executives, employees, managers and human resources.
- 'Managing School Bullying, Building Emotional and Social Resilience for Students, Bully Blocking Skills for Kids and Workplace Bullying for Schools.'
- Training for health professionals in treating victims of school and workplace bullying.

For further information on bullying and social resilience visit Evelyn's website at www.bullying.com.au.

Acknowledgments

My special thanks to Paul McCarthy, who inspired me to write a book on workplace bullying, and to my colleagues around the world. Thank you to my clients and workplace bullying support group, whom I can't name for confidential reasons, the inspiring international web support groups for victims of workplace bullying, and Shayne Mathieson who gave me feedback.

Although I've tried to quote references appropriately, some information was lost while I was ill and during extensive rewriting over ten years. I hope that those who weren't acknowledged will understand.

Thank you to Andrea Pilmear, Ann Wisniak, Anne Thompson, Barbara Guest, Barbara John, Bill Temple, Brian McAvoy, Charles Goulding, Charlotte Raynor, Charmine E.J. Härtel, David Field, David Griggs, Frederick Davidson, Gary Collis, George Halascz, George Norris, Guy Croyle, Hadyn Olsen, Helen Bourke, Helen Shardy, Helge Hoel, Jeff Lomas, Jo Murphy, Judy Bernshaw, Julie Ankers, Kalman Rubin, Kenneth Westhues, Kim Sawyer, Lori O'Keefe, Louis Waller, Mark Williams, Michael Sheehan, Michael Tunnecliffe, Michelle Barker, Naomi Raab, Noreen Tehrani, Pamela Lutgen-Sandvik, Pat Ferris, Patmalar Ambikapathy, Rabbi and Mrs Shimshon Yurkewicz, Rachel Yehuda, Rex Finch, Robyn Henderson, Rochelle Umansky, Ronnie Zohar, Robert Wood, Rueben and Vivienne Fried, Sally Jetson, Sam Horn, Sarah Cornally, Sarah Rey, Stale Einarson, Susan E. Shaub, Susan Marais Steiman, Susan Mclean, Tanya Goldenberg, Tim Field, Sara Vidal.

Bibliography

Adams, A. (1992). *Bullying at work: How to confront and overcome it.* London: Virago.

Babiak, P., & Hare, R.D. (2006). *Snakes in suits: When psychopaths go to work.* New York: Collins.

Clarke, J. (2005). *Working with monsters.* Sydney, Australia: Random House.

Crawshaw, L. (2007). *Taming the abrasive manager: How to end unnecessary roughness in the workplace.* Jossey-Bass Management Series.

Davenport, N., Schwartz, R.D., & Elliott, G.P. (1999). *Mobbing: Emotional abuse in the American workplace.* Ames, IO: Civil Society Publishing.

Einarsen, S., Hoel, H.Z.D., & Cooper, G.L. (2003). *Bullying and emotional abuse in the workplace.* London and New York: Taylor and Francis.

Felder, L. (1993). *Does someone at work treat you badly?* New York: Berkley Books.

Field, E.M. (2007). *Bully blocking.* Sydney, Australia: Finch.

Field, T. (1996). *Bully in sight.* UK: Success Unlimited.

Fineberg, L.S. (1996). *Teasing: Innocent fun or sadistic malice?* New Jersey: New Horizon Press.

Futterman, S. (2004). *When you work for a bully, assessing your options and taking action.* NJ: Croce Publishing Group

Graves, D. (2002). *Fighting back.* United Kingdom: McGraw Hill Professional.

Hare, R.D. (1999). *Without conscience, the disturbing world of psychopaths among us.* New York: Guilford Press.

Herman, J.M.D. (1997). *Trauma and recovery: The aftermath of violence from domestic abuse to political terror.* Basic Books.

Hockley, C. (2002). *Silent hell: workplace violence and bullying.* Adelaide, Australia: Peacock Publishers.

Horn, S. (2002). *Take the bully by the horns.* New York: St Martin's Press.

Hornstein, H. (1996). *Brutal bosses and their prey.* New York: Riverhead books.

Janoff-Bulman, R. (1992). *Shattered assumptions: Towards a new psychology of trauma.* New York: Free Press.

Marais, S., & Herman, M. (1997). *Corporate hyenas at work.* Pretoria: Kagiso Publishers.

Mathieson, S., Burns, J., & Hansen, M. (1998). *Safe and sound.* New Zealand: Top Drawer Consultants.

Namie, G., & Namie, R. (2009). *The bully at work.* USA: Source Books.

Olsen, H. (2005). *Workplace bullying and harassment.* CCH New Zealand Ltd

Randall, P. (1997). *Adult bullying: Perpetrators and victims.* London: Routledge.

Richards, H., & Freeman, S. (2002). *Bullying in the workplace: An occupational hazard.* Sydney, Australia: Harper Collins.

Solomon, M. (1990). *Working with difficult people.* USA: Prentice Hall.

Sutton, R. (2007). *The no asshole rule, building a civilized workplace and surviving one that isn't.* New York: Warner Business Plus, Hachette books.

Tehrani, N. (2001). *Building a culture of respect.* London & NY: Taylor Francis.

Wyatt, J., & Hare, C. (1997). Work abuse: How to recognize and survive it. Rochester, VT: Schenkman Books.

Lightning Source UK Ltd.
Milton Keynes UK
UKOW032303270213

206893UK00003B/37/P